# Managing Employees

## Management Sense versus Common Sense

By Fred Rogan

This book was previously published under the title
*What Your Employer Meant to Tell You When They Made You a Manager.*

Copyright © 2014 by Fred Rogan

Without limiting the rights under copyright reserved above,
no part of this publication may be reproduced, stored in or introduced into
a retrieval system, or transmitted, in any form or by any means
(electronic, mechanical, photocopying, recording, or otherwise),
without the prior written permission of both the copyright owner and
the publisher of this book.

Published by Aventine Press
55 East Emerson
Chula Vista CA, 91910
www.aventinepress.com

ISBN: 978-1-59330-737-0
Printed in the United States of America

ALL RIGHTS RESERVED

# Table of Contents

| | |
|---|---:|
| **Introduction** | 1 |
| **Section One** – How to Think and Behave Like a Manager | |
|     Management Sense and People Management | 5 |
|     "I am a New Manager, Help Me" | 7 |
|     A Family or a Team? | 11 |
|     Don't Give Yourself a Wedgie | 14 |
|     Selfless Management; an Oxymoron? | 16 |
|     Management Stewardship | 18 |
|     What Makes a Good Manager? | 20 |
|     The Infallibility of Management | 22 |
|     Don't Wonder Why You Wander | 24 |
|     How Are You Managing? | 26 |
|     Your Job? Helping Employees | 29 |
|     Small Change to Big Change | 32 |
|     Passive Aggressive Management | 37 |
|     No Sugar-Honey-Ice tea; No Profanity | 39 |
|     Irrational Escalation | 41 |
|     What Judges Think | 43 |
|     Putting Off Procrastination | 45 |
|     Mis-placed Loyalty | 48 |
| **Section Two** – How to Create an Environment in Which Your Employees Will Want to Work | |
|     The Poetry of Retention | 53 |

| | |
|---|---|
| Issuing Good Instructions to Employees | 56 |
| Clear Communication | 58 |
| Orientation to Departmental Orientation | 60 |
| Promoting a Training Culture | 63 |
| Steps to Employee Training | 65 |
| Employees Expect Expectations | 67 |
| Management Terrorism | 69 |
| Just Kidding, Not Really | 71 |
| PITA People | 73 |
| Bad Attitudes | 75 |
| Dysfunctional Self-Selection Cycle | 77 |
| Harassment – Don't Do It or Allow It | 79 |
| Retaliation – Don't Do It or Allow It Either | 81 |
| Things You Should Never Say or Do to an Employee (or Applicant) | 82 |
| Evaluating Employee Performance | 85 |
| Taking the Hesitation Out of Documentation | 89 |
| Verbal Versus Written Warnings | 94 |
| Make a Note of It | 96 |
| Termination of Employment – It Happens | 98 |
| The Termination Meeting | 100 |

**Section Three** – People Selection

| | |
|---|---|
| Management Sense and People Selection | 105 |
| Why Making Good Hires is Critical | 106 |
| Hiring Procedures – Got Any? | 107 |
| Hire the Best People You Can Find | 109 |
| The Maximum on Minimum Qualifications | 111 |

| | |
|---|---|
| The Benefits of Experience | 115 |
| What Do I Ask During an Interview? | 117 |
| Hiring a Manager is Not Like Hiring Anyone Else | 122 |
| The Advantages of Job Posting | 126 |
| Internal Transfers – Don't Pass the Lemon | 129 |
| How to Avoid Hiring the Wrong Person | 131 |

**Section Four** – Application

| | |
|---|---|
| Employment Laws | 135 |
| Putting All of This to Work | 137 |
| **Endnotes** | 139 |
| **About the Author** | 141 |

*"People will work longer and harder for good management and poor pay than they will for poor management and good pay."* Fred Rogan, human resources practitioner

# Introduction

This book is for first-line supervisors, managers, department heads, directors, vice presidents and CEOs; in other words, all levels of management. Many people in management have been promoted into these jobs because they are good at what they do; they are subject matter experts in their field. In health care, a hardworking, competent nurse is made a head nurse because he is good at nursing. In banking, a high-performing commercial lender is made head of the commercial lending department because she understands commercial lending. In higher education, a faculty member in the History Department is made chair of the department because that faculty member is highly regarded for teaching and publishing.

In all of the above examples, these are high-performing, competent people who have been promoted. However, what they may not have knowledge of, and what their employer may not train them in, is the management of other employees. Many of the people in these positions believe that common sense is all that is necessary for people to manage other people. When you think about it, even that is not good common sense.

Aubrey Daniels, in *Bringing Out the Best in People,* makes the point that there is too much reliance on common sense in management.[1] I have observed managers rely solely on common sense and consequently make some very bad management decisions. Some managers use no sense at all but that is another issue.

Daniels says that when you use your common sense, you are doing what makes sense to you, not necessarily what makes sense in a management context.[2] Your common sense is not good enough when making decisions in the workplace. You must develop what I call Management Sense. You do that by reading management books like this one, attending training sessions, working with a good management mentor and then, and most importantly, by applying what you've learned.

Management Sense is a body of knowledge and behaviors for application in the manager–employee relationship that includes good business practices, good employment practices, employment law, courtesy, civility and bits of psychology and sociology. My intent is to touch on each of those areas and hopefully help you develop your Management Sense.

To be effective, this book (or any book on management) must be read and then incorporated into your management style. The goal is to give the head nurse, the head of the commercial lending department, the faculty chair and you a sense of what is expected in your role as a manager and how to fulfill that role.

With all of the demands managers have on their lives, reading this book should require as little time as possible. Therefore, the chapters are succinct and I have made ample use of lists in practically every chapter to facilitate learning. The book is arranged as follows:

- Section one offers ideas on how you might think and behave as a manager, things you need to do or not do; say or not say.
- Section two provides suggestions that can help you create an environment in which employees will want to work. Retention and engagement of employees is a much overlooked element of a manager's job.
- Section three gives you some very practical and helpful ideas for people selection – another critical element of a manager's job.
- Section four briefly addresses tying all of this information together.

Remember as you read that nothing in this book is intended to be legal advice or to take the place of legal advice. If you have a question regarding legal matters, consult the attorney that represents your organization in employment matters.

# Section One

# How to Think and Behave Like a Manager

# Management Sense and People Management

If it were not for people, being a manager would be a cinch. Maybe you are a manager who manages only ideas or things, if so; this book will help you in future jobs where you do manage people. Most people would agree that managing people is much harder than managing ideas or things. Ideas and things do not talk back, have attendance or performance problems, and they don't file lawsuits.

Good managers can save organizations money. Less effective managers can cost money in turnover, poor productivity and in causing grievances and EEOC complaints. But good managers are rare. I mean the kind of managers that people really want to work for and the kind of managers that really get things done. The kind of managers who are not threatened by good employees and the kind of managers who are selfless enough to help employees develop to their fullest potential.

Good managers are not born and if you believe that as I do, that means you also believe that good managers can be developed. I am talking about developing the behavior exhibited by managers when managing employees. Good managers are people who have learned and/or are mentally mature enough to understand that their behavior as a manager makes a difference in the work-lives of their employees. These managers are self-aware and self-controlled enough to use the appropriate behavior or are able to modify their behavior based on the situation because they understand the impact their behavior can have on employees.

A manager is not just an employee who gets to tell other employees what to do. Being a manager is more complex, more nuanced than that. There are specific KSAs (knowledge, skills and abilities) that a manager must have. This section will cover some of the more nuanced aspects of being a manager as well as some big-picture items. When you are at work in your job as a manager, you are in the proverbial fishbowl. Employees are examining and discussing your behavior: every mood, decision, outburst and pronouncement. This section will help you recognize your behaviors that affect employees, how your employees may perceive you as a result of your behaviors and how you might want to change some of those behaviors.

For Your Consideration:

a. What were the defining behaviors of the best manager for whom you have ever worked?
b. What were the defining behaviors of the worst manager for whom you have ever worked?

## "I am a New Manager; Help Me"

While I was working in Human Resources at a large teaching hospital, the Director of the Laboratory called me and said that Jane, a Medical Technologist, had applied for and been promoted to be manager of the reference lab, a large section of the lab with about 15 employees. She asked if I would explain some of the administrative responsibilities of a manager with Jane. I met with Jane and learned that, while she had been a Medical Technologist, with an excellent record for almost 20 years, this was her first time to supervise employees. We went over what she needed from me, and I wished her the best in her new role. At that time the hospital did not have a training program for new managers.

About six months later, Jane came to my office unannounced and collapsed in tears. She had had enough of employee excuses, employee problems and the interpersonal headaches that can come with supervising a group of people. She said to cut her pay, do whatever was needed, but put her back in her old job with no more responsibility for managing people. Working with the Director of the Laboratory, we put Jane back in her old job.

Jane was frustrated to the breaking point because she had no background for dealing with all of the issues that employees present. Jane was an excellent medical technologist but had no management experience or training.

So where do you start if you are a new manager? You may ask, "What if I am a new manager like Jane? What if I have just been promoted to manage my former peers like Jane?" These are questions that I am frequently asked and they are good questions. Here are the answers I would offer:

1. Inquire as to whether your organization provides any training for managers, take it and learn from it.
2. Find out what your employees do. If job descriptions exist, read them; if they don't, write them – that is a good way to learn what your people do. There are sometimes undesirable tasks that employ-

ees have that can intentionally fall through the cracks when a manager changes.

3. Find out how your employees describe the culture. Then, try to determine how it became that way. It is necessary to know some history of your organization and your department – just don't become stuck in the muck.
4. Review your employees' previous performance appraisals (assuming they exist and assuming they were done accurately in the first place) and any documentation that may be in the file. Review your employees' files, a frequently overlooked source of information. Employees with problems should not get a clean slate just because a manager has changed. Some new managers tell me that, trying to sound magnanimous, but it is not really a good idea. Remember that the co-workers of the employee with problems will know if that employee gets a clean slate, and they may then think of you more in terms of cowardice than magnanimity. Read the appraisals and the files objectively and develop an informed opinion, but respect the work that may have been done by the previous manager.
5. Review any business processes that are in writing. You need to learn how things work, how things are done and have a good command of this knowledge. Become a subject-matter expert in how your department works as soon as you can.
6. Sit down with your employees and ask each one to tell you what works well and what does not work so well in your area. There may be low-hanging fruit here – processes that you can repair right away. Plus, it is good to know how your employees feel about processes as well as what those processes are. Even if you cannot change a process that is disliked, you can show appropriate empathy when the time comes.
7. Sit down with each employee and tell him/her what you will expect in terms of behavior and performance, and then describe to each employee how much of what you just told him/her will be used to evaluate performance. Too few managers tell employees from the outset what behavior and performance expectations will form the basis of the performance appraisal.
8. One of the most common problems that new managers face is realizing that the former manager was not accurate with what was writ-

ten in performance appraisals or that no documentation of poor performance was completed. Consequently, you are faced with an employee who has performance problems but who has a file that does not reflect that fact. You have to start the process, and you do so by explaining to the employee what your expectations are and where his/her performance fails to meet those expectations. You give the employee reasonable time to make corrections, then follow up and address the performance deficits with the intent of helping the employee correct the problem.

9. Listen to your employees and take notes. Find out who they are and what they want to be. Listen well.
10. If you have a Human Resources function, use them as a resource to find out any history or anything else you may need to know about your department.

And the second question: What if you have been promoted to manage your former peers?

1. Meet with each employee and acknowledge that this may be an awkward situation but that you will do your best to become a good manager. You already know what issues are important to your former co-workers, so do not ignore these.
2. Explain that you need each employee's support, ask for their support, and thank them for their support. Explain that you will be available to support them in every way that you can. Know that you will not freely receive the support of each and every employee; some of them you will have to win over by your performance.
3. You must accept and acknowledge to your employees that relationships may have to change. Relationships will be different because you are no longer one of the boys/girls. This is the toughest part for newly promoted managers to deal with. It is a balancing act between your employees not thinking you have become too big for your britches, and you not changing your behavior at all. There absolutely has to be a change in how you relate to the people that you now supervise. It does not mean that you are too big for your britches, but it does mean that you have a new job with new authority and responsibilities. You cannot show favoritism by continuing your old relation-

ships in which you probably spent more time with some co-workers than with others. You must now have a very finely tuned balance in those relationships so that you spend equal amounts of time with each of your employees (and, yes, this will mean that any after–hours relationships with employees must change as well).

It will be very important for you as a new manager to develop your Management Sense and to use it. Your success in management will depend upon it.

For your consideration:

a.  What is the hardest part of being a new manager?
b.  What is the hardest part of being a manager of your former peers?

## A Family or a Team?

In our post-modern world the word family has become difficult to define. It has taken on a much broader meaning that has been politicized to some degree. But, we typically think of a family as a group of people related by some kind of marriage or by blood. Regardless of our definition of family, my point is that there is a difference between a family and a team.

One element of a family is that it is a group of people who care for and support each other. Hopefully you have that element in your team at work. But, if a member of a family is not performing their family duties, i.e., taking out the garbage, while disciplinary action may be taken, a family and a team will take different approaches to the problem.

A team is made up of individuals who are selected to be a part of the team because they possess the knowledge, skills and abilities necessary to carry out their assigned duties. To use a sports analogy; on a baseball team the shortstop requires good fielding skills, quick reflexes and a good arm. If the short-stop is not making the plays, he/she is coached, given extra practice, etc., until the problem is corrected. If the problem is not corrected, the short-stop is traded down or off of the team. While families do not treat poor performers like that (generally), in the workplace, we should. This is the most compelling argument that the workplace functions more like a team than a family.

Families work best when instead of worrying about who is doing the most work around the house, everyone tries to do the most they can do and do their best at what they do. Good teams share this attribute. Good team members are concerned enough about the team that they make sure they do their job and help any other team member they see who may need help. The point is not the individual but the team.

Obviously there are attributes of both families and of teams that we would want to have in the workplace. Here is a non-exhaustive breakdown:

Family attributes that we want in the workplace:

1. A caring, supportive group of people
2. Every person attempting to do his/her best
3. Always doing what is best for the family
4. Honesty in dealing with others

Team attributes that we want in the workplace:

1. All of the family attributes plus:
2. The right knowledge, skills and abilities in our members
3. Coaches (managers) who develop our team members
4. Coaches who makes the necessary personnel changes to keep the team operating at peak efficiency
5. Coaches who can make the tough decisions to keep the team together
6. Coaches who understand the game and can win

You can see from the above lists that as far as the team is concerned, the coach makes a big difference. On your team at work, if you are the supervisor, then you are the coach, you are not the mom or the dad. The rest of this book is about making you a good coach at work, about developing your Management Sense.

Keep in mind, the word family throughout this chapter is being used in the metaphorical sense. I am a big believer that (unless it is a family business) hiring family members is fraught with problems (and that is sometimes the case even in family businesses) and should be avoided. The problems that may occur are:

1. Inappropriate pillow talk (particularly where it is both spouses that are employed)
2. If you have to take negative action against one, you wind up with two disgruntled employees
3. If one leaves, the other may as well and you have lost two employees.

It does sound strange to me to hear a CEO or manager describe the workplace as one big, happy family. That metaphor is just not sustainable. Ultimately, the concept of a team is more sustainable, applicable and appropriate for the workplace. However, we have to remember that it is people who make up both teams and families and there are attributes of both entities that are relevant for the workplace.

For your consideration:

a) Can you think of additional team or family attributes desirable in the workplace?
b) If you have been thinking of or talking about your workgroup as a family, what can you do to make the switch to thinking and talking about them as a team?

## Don't Give Yourself a Wedgie

You are a member of the management team; the management team includes you and everyone else in a management capacity, top to bottom, in the organization. It follows, then, that everyone in management at your organization is on the same management team. You may have different levels of management, but I doubt that you have different teams of management.

That leads us to the next point: There is only one pronoun that you can use when you are referring to management, and that pronoun is "we."[3] For example, let's say you receive a decision (with which you do not agree) from management two or three levels above you. You then tell your employees that "they" have done it to us again. By saying this, you are driving a wedge between you and your management. In the eyes of your employees, you are becoming a victim of management rather than being a member of management.

An alternative response to share with your employees would be, "Management has made a decision, and this is what we are doing". You may or may not have been in on the decision- making process, but the implied message to your employees is that you support the decision. That is as it should be; everyone on the team supports the team.

What if you do not agree with the decision? Voicing to your employees your disagreement with a management decision only harms you. Instead, go to your boss, go to HR, write a letter to your CEO to express your disagreement but do not, in front of your employees, drive a wedge between you and your management. That is a wedgie that is uncomfortable for everyone involved.

Another way you may give yourself a wedgie is when you do not filter something your managers says to you about an employee that reports to you. If your manager says something unflattering about one of your employees, filter it! Do not repeat to the employee what your boss said.

Maybe your boss should not have made the comment but you make things worse by repeating it. The person that hurts the most is you.

Does the above sound like it comes from the Pollyanna School of Management? Perhaps, but it is still a standard to which we should aspire. All of us have most likely been guilty at some point in our career of driving that wedge between our management and ourselves. Think about it the next time a management decision (with which you do not agree) comes down, and then craft your communication to employees so that it is clear which team you are on.

For your consideration:

a. Why shouldn't a manager bond with employees by referring to upper management as "they"?
b. What if a manager doesn't feel she can go to her boss to express disagreement with a management decision?

# Selfless Management; an Oxymoron?

One of the most important traits of a good manager is selflessness. Not many employees think of managers as being selfless, but if you think about it, managers are charged with the care of other people. If you manage people, you are therefore called upon to have a greater degree of selflessness.

Having been a father of three children, I can attest that babies are the least selfless creatures on earth. However, as they grow and develop, most children grow out of considering themselves as the center of the universe (pity that not all do). So, for most people, by the time they reach their child-bearing and child-rearing years, they should be selfless enough that they consistently put the needs of their offspring ahead of their own needs.

Severe weather was bearing down on the town in which Roy worked. He came out of his office and said to Jane, his Administrative Assistant, "It's getting bad out there, I'm going home." He did not mention to Jane whether she could leave, take cover or what. Jane was naturally hurt and dismayed by Roy's lack of concern for her. This is an actual example of a manager who never grew out of considering himself the center of the universe.

The growth-progression is that as managers we should be mature enough in our work-life and our relationships to those we manage that we can sublimate our egos as we manage and develop those under our supervision. (Be careful not to take this analogy too far! Managers are not the parents, and employees are not the children.)

Here are some examples of how you can put your employee's needs before yours:

1. Make yourself accessible and available to employees, even when you don't feel like doing so.

2. Think of your employees' needs at work as you think of your own.
3. Ensure that each employee knows his/her job and that you give constructive feedback on a regular basis – as in daily.
4. Share your expertise with employees.
5. Do all that you can to develop your employees, even if it makes you feel vulnerable because you have an employee who may be smarter than you or who has a stronger work ethic than you do.
6. Be generous with your time in listening to and working with employees.
7. Ensure that employees have the resources needed to perform their jobs even if it means you give something up.
8. Do not put yourself first when planning salary increases.
9. Do not put yourself first when planning time off.

Whether you are the CEO or a first-line manager, you are not the most important person – make sure you behave accordingly. Don't act like a self-centered baby. Check your ego at the door when coming to work and give yourself unselfishly to those whom you manage.

For your consideration:

a. How does a manager make the leap from being self-centered to being other-centered?
b. Why is it important for managers to be other-centered (at least at work)?

# Management Stewardship

Stewardship is the responsible use of resources. There is a kind of management stewardship that we need to practice every day that we are at work.

Management stewardship is the appropriate use of our time, talents and resources in the pursuit of meeting the goals of your organization. The following are examples of what might be considered good management stewardship:

1. Creating and maintaining an environment in which people want to work so you do not create turnover. You have to actively manage this; it does not just happen. This will be discussed further in subsequent chapters.
2. Being available to and communicating with those whom you manage so you do not waste their time because they cannot get answers. When your employees cannot get answers from you, they are frustrated by the hurdle you represent, and you are viewed as a drain on the organization because you do not value their time – which your employees know is money.
3. Developing employees so that their current jobs are enriched or so that they feel they have the opportunity to move onward and upward. This means giving employees good training and enriching their work whenever possible.
4. Applying your own policies and internal governance in a consistent and even-handed manner so your employees know they work for a fair manager. As in, do not show favoritism and know your organization's policies and apply them even-handedly.
5. Promptly taking corrective action with any employee whose performance/behavior is not meeting your expectations so that he knows he is not doing a good job and why.
6. Making decisions that reflect a prudent use of the organization's human and material resources. Be conscious of cost when using people and resources and use them as if the cost were coming out of your pocket.

7. Giving a raise or promotion to those employees whose performance warrants a raise or promotion (when the time comes) so that they know they will be rewarded for doing a good job. Admittedly, this is not easy to do in many organizations.

Engaging in these behaviors on a regular basis will be evidence of your having good Management Sense. You will also set an example of stewardship of your organization's resources that you want your employees to follow.

For your consideration:

a. Why is stewardship an important component of a manager's role?
b. What are other ways managers can be good stewards of an organizations resources?

# What Makes a Good Manager?

Good managers may be born with some of the traits that make them good managers and the Management Sense that we are talking about includes some of those traits. However, being a good manager, and having and using Management Sense is more than relying on the gifts with which you are born. A good manager must be aware of what it takes to be a good manager and consciously work on developing those traits as well as the ones that are absent at birth. Some of the traits you must develop to be a good manager are:

1. Self-Awareness – Be aware of when your emotions are elevated and make the necessary adjustments so that it appears you are in control of yourself. How can you manage others if you cannot manage yourself?
2. Extroversion – This means being able to talk to people, being able to talk to people when it is an uncomfortable, perhaps confrontational situation and being able to draw other people out of their inwardness when necessary.
3. Good listening skills – Good listening is very self-sacrificial. It means holding what you want to say until you have heard everything the other person wants to say and listening and believing that what the other person has to say could matter.
4. Subject matter expertise – Part of being a good manager is being a technical advisor. You must be a subject matter expert in your field. If your employees realize that they cannot come to you for answers to questions, you will quickly lose credibility.
5. Balance – Most of your employees want a balanced life. They will want you to have a balanced life so that they know you know what that is, and they can have hopes of having one as well.
6. Objectivity – Objectivity usually (in this context) means fair and fair usually means balanced, all sides being heard or having the opportunity to present. Your being objective means not rushing to judgment, being aware of your preconceived biases, and being open to all information no matter where it takes you.

These are some of the most important traits of managers with good Management Sense. These traits are not developed overnight, and, with some, you have to recognize that you don't have it before you can work on its development.

For your consideration:

a. Can you think of other traits of a good manager?
b. Think of the person with whom you have worked who you think had the best Management Sense – what was his/her best or strongest trait?

## The Infallibility of Management

"Incapable of making errors" – that is what Webster's New Collegiate says regarding the word "infallible." Is management infallible?

To make an error or not – that is, to be right or wrong – you first have to make a decision. Making decisions is one of the most important functions of management, maybe the most important function. Management has to make decisions almost by the moment about budgets, people, processes, policies and situations that occur. It could be said that the degree to which a manager is successful is the degree to which a manager is able to make good decisions.

I worked with Sue, a manager who had a very hard time making decisions. Sue over analyzed everything and never seemed to know when enough was enough. She had a difficult time bringing closure to any decision. Part of her problem was that she was in a position that was over her head. She was over-employed; she was in a job for which her knowledge, skills and abilities were inadequate for the decisions that faced her on a daily basis. Putting her in this job was a mistake that her manager made, but it affected all who reported to her and who depended on her decision making skills (refer to the chapter on How to Hire a Manager).

But part of Sue's inability to make a decision also came from her fear of making a mistake. Her lack of confidence in her own decision-making ability profoundly affected the way she was viewed by her employees. They saw her as an incompetent, insecure person.

There is an expectation by those being managed that management will make decisions. That is how things get done – managers make decisions, then employees execute their delegated duties and the decisions are carried out. The management decisions that are made must be based on input from employees as well as the manager's experience, education and knowledge of the current, relevant facts. Once the facts are gathered, analyzed and filtered through the manager's frame of reference, the decision can be made.

But is there an expectation that management will be infallible? Do employees really think that management will never make an error in making a decision? No, in fact, the expectation is just the opposite, that management will make mistakes. Whether or not a manager sees him/herself as a person capable of making mistakes, employees do because employees understand that people make mistakes.

The response of employees to management mistakes depends on the behavior of the manager after making a mistake. Inappropriate behaviors by a manager following a mistake include:

1. Not learning from your mistake – repeating mistakes over and over is embarrassing and yes, it is stupid (I hate to use that S-word but…). Ask for help if you have to, but do something so you learn what you are doing wrong.
2. Not acknowledging that there was a mistake – thereby committing yet another mistake. Employees know when a manager has made a mistake. It is as obvious as the nose on your face. Admit when you make a mistake; own your mistake; ask for help; apologize, ask for forgiveness if necessary. The good news is that at least you made a decision, even if you did make a mistake.
3. Blaming it on someone or something else – in other words, it was not the manager's fault. This may be worse than the first reaction because it involves deception; you lose credibility and respect if you do this.

Admit when you have made a mistake (but at the same time, congratulations on having made a decision, even if it was a mistake). People have an immense capacity for forgiveness when a sincere admission of a mistake is made. To admit mistakes is honest, transparent and what employees expect you to do. Management is not infallible and, for that matter, neither is your Management Sense.

For your consideration:

a. What are the best and worst aspects of making a work decision?
b. After having made a mistake how could you have better handled the aftermath?

## Don't Wonder Why You Wander

Over a period of several months, while I was working in HR in banking, I received several reports of mischief, disagreements among employees and just general chaos from the loan review department. Having the sharp eye that I do for management problems, I decided to investigate. What I found, with very little utilization of my investigatory skills, was that Glen, the department manager, would come in each morning, go into his office, shut the door and not come out except for lunch and breaks. For any one of his 12 employees to see Glen, they had to set up a meeting with him through his secretary. That was not very smart, it was very inefficient, and it is not a good way to manage people.

To be an effective manager, you have to be out and about, in and around the people whom you manage. You need to be very accessible and to do a good job of listening to those you supervise. You have no doubt heard of MBWA: Management By Wandering Around. This is more than just wandering; it is wandering with a goal in mind – gathering information, helping to spread your vision, caring about people.[4] Here are some tips to make your MBWA more effective[5]:

1. Take time to sit with people and find out who they are. Why are they here? How did they get here? What are their interests? What can you do to help them do their jobs? Knowing the people that you work with helps to develop a climate of mutual trust and respect, and it is critical to getting everyone committed to a common purpose.
2. Let your employees know that you are seeking their feedback and then be ready to listen and hear. If you are defensive or discount the feedback, it will have a serious chilling effect on receiving feedback in the future. Ask questions when you receive feedback to be sure you understand and to show interest, but not in a defensive way. Acting on and incorporating suggestions received from all levels makes a very productive environment.
3. MBWA means accessibility. Even when you are not wandering, be available to answer questions. If employees feel as though they can-

not approach your inner-sanctum, you will be isolated from the very people you depend on. Staying available and in touch creates a more effective organization.

4. As you are out and about, give compliments. Think, right now, when was the last time you gave a compliment to an employee for a job well done? Make a point to give a deserved compliment every day to someone who works for you. Tell them how you feel about what they have done and encourage them.
5. Remember:

    a. Everyone in your group is an individual; speak to them as individuals.
    b. Go out of your way to receive feedback.
    c. As you wander, be a good listener. Stop what you are doing and listen. Remember, you cannot listen while you are talking.
    d. Good managers believe that intelligence is widely distributed among the employee population; harvest that intelligence.

Glen never wandered and that was a mistake. Just his presence might have prevented some of the problems that ultimately made him look like he did not have good Management Sense.

For your consideration:

a. As a manager, what advantages are there to you, to be out among your employees?
b. How do you make your employees perceive your interest in them as sincere?

## How Are You Managing?

There are employment laws and policies and procedures we have to be mindful of but a large part of managing is simply common courtesy. Many times, I have observed, it is rude or inconsiderate behavior by managers that causes the unpleasantness in the workplace such as charges of discrimination, poor morale and turnover. Correcting this poor management behavior costs literally nothing but can pay great dividends.

Management's role is not to be served by employees but to serve employees. That may be a very surprising statement to you because you have seen many managers treat employees as if the employees are their personal assistants. Unless "personal assistant" is the employee's job title, that is not what the employee is there to do.

Instead, managers must spend a significant amount of time making sure that employees have what they need in order to do their job successfully and that includes a good work environment. Let's see how you are managing:

1. With whom are you spending time?

Do you spend time both on a formal and an informal basis with those who report to you? Spend time listening to your employees and meeting with them so that *their* issues are the topic of the meeting. Then listen; you don't have to agree or disagree, just listen. Spend time informally with your employees; have a pot-luck lunch or go out to lunch (but not with the same employee all the time).

2. How do you communicate?

Do you communicate everything by e-mail? That certainly has its place, but do not overdo it. There are times when you must speak to people face to face. Do not set a pattern of giving the good news in person and saving the bad news for e-mail. Use good judgment in the use of e-mails to employees.

3. What kind of mood are you in?

Are you a moody manager? Universally, employees hate moodiness in managers. Think about it: you also would rather avoid the unpredictability of a moody manager. It is easy to fall into a bad mood when things do not suit you. However, when you are a manager of people, you have to leave your bad mood at the door. Your job is to set the tone for the workplace, and no one wants to have you share your bad mood with them. Hopefully, if you are moody, you know it and will do something about it. If not, I hope someone tells you in a nice way so it doesn't put you in a bad mood.

4. How are your social skills?

Your employees are adults; they are not your children, and they have an expectation that they are going to be treated with a certain level of civility. That means cordial greetings, cordial responses to greetings, polite requests, and giving full attention when someone is speaking to you. It is rude to be engaged in some other activity when someone is trying to speak to you.

5. What example do you set?

If you subscribe to the concept that a major role of a manager's job is to support employees, you would want to set a good example for your employees in your work habits. Your arrival, departure, quality and quantity of work should all be examples you would want your employees to follow. The manner in which you treat people would be the most important example that you would want to set for employees.

6. Do you pay attention to your subordinates?

Do you have some idea of what is going on in your employees' lives? Once people are hired, there is no law that says you cannot ask about an employee's spouse, children, hobbies or interests. (To use that information as the basis of an employment decision might be risky, so let's talk before doing that.) In other words, it is a good thing to know your people. Learn the names of their children and their spouse. Ask them about their weekend, etc.

7. Respect your employees.

Respect their time. Don't call unnecessary meetings. When you do have meetings, cover what you need to cover and then let everyone get back to work. If you have an appointment with one of your employees, be punctual or let him/her know that you are running late and will need to reschedule. Your people are working for you, and they will see your wasting of their time as a wasting of resources. Respect their egos. No one wants to be discounted or marginalized. We all have a place in the hierarchy, but we all want to feel as if we are special, and that we make a unique contribution.

8. Do you challenge your subordinates?

Most employees want to be challenged. They want to grow, to learn and to do things that stimulate their thinking. To challenge your employees, you must be an effective delegator.

9. Do you allow your subordinates to challenge you?

How much tolerance do you have for disagreement? Letting your employees challenge your decisions is tough sometimes but it is also a way for you and your employees to grow together, a way to avoid mistakes, and a way to get the best ideas on the table. Being totally comfortable with being challenged is the true mark of a self-confident manager with good Management Sense.

As a manager, you would want your own boss to be guided by the above points in how he/she treats you. It is a comfort to know that the simplest rules, like the Golden Rule, always make the most sense, even when we work in an over-complicated world.

For your consideration:

a. How important do you think it is for managers to be civil to employees? Why?
b. What do you think about the idea of it being a manager's role to serve employees?

## Your Job? Helping Employees

When I first went to work at a bank in the late 1980s, my first role in Human Resources was as corporate benefits manager. At that time the bank had about 6000 employees and, at certain times of the year we would send benefits communications material out to all 6000. This was a very paper intensive process and a very complicated mail-out. There were usually 5-7 pieces that had to be stuffed and several contained actual employee information, so each piece had to be carefully collated by hand to get it in the right envelope, etc.

My staff of 5 employees was solely responsible for this mail-out. To shorten the time it took, I would stuff envelopes with everyone else. We would work for days, order in food and generally have a great time talking, laughing and stuffing envelopes.

I had lunch with one of those employees almost 25 years later and she brought up the fun she had stuffing envelopes all those years ago. What I did not realize back then was that our performing this manual labor together had the effect of creating a great team-building exercise. We learned more about each other personally; we talked about how we could work better together; we generated new ideas and just generally had a very good bonding experience. I wish I could say that I had planned this team – building experience, but all I had set out to do was to help my employees complete a very labor-intensive project.

One of the most overlooked roles for managers is the role of helping employees to do their jobs. What better way to build a team than to work with them on their tasks, help them do their jobs while getting to know them? When you engage in team-building exercises, it begs for the sports analogy that puts you in the role of coach. This is worth further consideration.

Your role is not only to supervise, but also to coach. Let's look at those two words. Generally, we think the word "supervise" means to watch over, and it may have some negative connotations. To supervise someone means to keep them in line, to keep them doing what they are supposed to be doing. Hopefully, that is not all you are doing as a manager.

To coach has a much more positive connotation. When we think of a coach, we think of someone who is going to help us get better at something, someone who will help us over rough spots, and someone who will help us become a winner. That is a much better description of what we ought to be doing with our employees. Coach employees, help them get better at their jobs and help them over rough spots in their jobs.

As a manager (coach), you must remember that employees are not there solely to help you do your job. Your employees have their own jobs, and at times it is part of your job to do what you can to help them, to coach them. How can you do this?

1. Give adequate training. Make sure employees know what to do and how to do it. Don't take this for granted.
2. Give adequate resources. Very few people have everything they want, but try to get everything your employees need to do their job. Don't withhold resources.
3. Cut red tape. That is what it is there for—to be cut. Maybe we can't eliminate all of the red tape, but when there is a matter that needs to be expedited and you can do it, just do it. Use your clout, your connections, and your charm.
4. Be the subject matter expert. Employees come to you for answers to technical questions—you need to keep up to date in your field, know what is happening in your area and be able to answer questions or to find answers to questions.
5. Make decisions. Whether it is on internal processes or on larger issues, analyze the data and then make a decision. Part of your job as a manager is to be a decision maker.
6. Define processes. Who does what, when? Make sure everyone knows and write it down so it is consistent and can be covered if someone is out.
7. Redesign processes. Are internal processes a burden to your employees? Take a look at how your area does business; if you are doing things that no longer make sense, change it.

8. Lend a hand. Is there a big job coming up, or is someone out? An extra set of hands is sometimes needed and having you in there working with everyone else can be a big morale booster (assuming you actually make a contribution).
9. Ask your employees what you can do to help. This does a lot: It lets employees know you care and you will learn details about how your employees' jobs work or don't work.
10. Listen to your employees. Stop what you are doing, look at the person and listen to what is being said. Just knowing that you know what is going on can be a help to employees and they may not feel that you know unless they tell you. This means stop e-mailing; take no calls; no texting; just listen to the person in front of you.

Helping your employees to do their job will make you a better manager and will make your employees more likely to follow, more likely to do a good job, and more likely to stay. Way to go, coach!

For your consideration:

a. What is your ratio of supervising to coaching and how do you think it needs to change?
b. What changes can you make in your management style to become more of a coach?

# Small Change to Big Change

*Change is the law of life. And those who look only to the past or present are certain to miss the future.* John F. Kennedy, former president

*Change in all things is sweet.* Aristotle, Greek philosopher

*Bebop was about change, about evolution. It wasn't about standing still and becoming safe. If anybody wants to keep creating, they have to be about change.* Miles Davis, jazz musician

Change is happening every day. There is change in the usual churn as people come and go. There will be change as technologies influence the way we work. There will be change as one day follows the next. Change is a constant, it never ends.

I was hired as a consultant for the local office of a large blood bank. They suspected that some of their employees in the apheresis area were encouraging their donors to contact the national office to complain about some changes that had been made in the apheresis process. The local office did not want their employees doing that. Apheresis donors are people who come in on a regular basis to donate plasma; they are in the chair for 2-3 hours and develop close relationships with the employees.

I interviewed management and asked them when the apheresis employees had been informed of the changes and if their input into the changes had been allowed. They told me that there was a memo to the employees asking for their input. When I saw the memo, I saw that it was not addressed to the apheresis employees, and the management employees it was addressed to were told by the memo what changes were going to take place.

I asked if there were another time the employees were informed and was told there was a meeting held where the changes were announced. When I saw the meeting roster, I saw that no apheresis employees were at the meeting.

So the bottom line is that changes that affected these employees' jobs were made without consulting the employees (the average tenure of these employees was over 15 years, so they knew their jobs), and they found out about the changes when a general announcement was made. The employees felt like management was not going to seek their opinion, so they used their donors as their advocates.

Even when it is well communicated, employees often are not thrilled at the prospect of change. Your job is to help ease their anxiety, to help them understand the need for the change. To do this, I offer some insight into employee thinking (after all, I am one).

Here are some examples of how employees might think regarding change:

Employee comment: I know my job now; if it changes, I will have to learn it all over.
Manager response: If you have to learn your job all over that will be a good learning experience that helps you grow as a person and enhances your value to the organization.

Employee comment: I may have to work more/harder because of the change.
Manager response: Working more/harder helps the day go by faster and you are making a greater contribution, thereby making yourself more valuable as an employee.

Employee comment: I will have to work more/harder just to learn the changes.
Manager response: Working more/harder to learn a new way is challenging and positive.

Employee comment: This change threatens my job security.
Manager response: Your job security may be heightened if you can show that you are flexible, adapt easily and are not averse to more/harder work.

Employee comment: The people (friends) I interact with may change.
Manager response: The people you work with are great but there are other great people here that you have not had the opportunity to meet or to work with.

Employee comment: The change was not my idea; therefore, it cannot be good.
Manager response: I want your ideas; please give me your thoughts about the changes. I recognize that other people are capable of having good ideas.

Employee comment: This is the way we have always done things.
Manager response: We may have always done things a certain way but we have a new leader (new technology, new situation, etc.), and that means things will change; you will want to be a contributing part of the success.

Back in the early '90s, the bank I was with decided that, to grow, we had to increase market share, and to do that we had to totally, unreservedly embrace a sales culture. This bank did not, at the time, have a strong sales culture. But rather than start by training employees in sales, we subjected every employee in the bank to a three-hour seminar on change, just the concept of change, what it is, why it is good, how to embrace it.

The change seminar worked; the employees knew the winds were about to shift. When we introduced the sales component, scorecards, goals, incentives, etc., most of the employees were much more receptive to the change. Those who weren't willing to change eventually left, but that is how change is. You need to accept it or move on.

Change constantly affects us as individuals, and frequently we do not like it. As managers, we need to be aware of organizational change issues and how we can facilitate when change is necessary.

Sometimes change efforts are not successful. A Human Resources textbook I have used lists some of the reasons why change efforts can fail:[6]

1. Not establishing a sense of urgency. There is a reason for the change and the reason is important. *We knew if we did not create a sales culture we could not survive as an independent bank.*
2. Not creating a powerful coalition to guide the effort. The right people have to support the change and direct the change. *The bank did form a coalition that was made up of people who had the interest and the means to introduce the sales culture.*

3. Lacking leaders who have a vision. Someone has to be able to see what the change is going to look like. *The executive management team had members who had been at banks that did have a strong sales culture and they knew what it looked like.*
4. Lacking leaders who communicate the vision. Someone has to be able to explain to others what the change looks like. *The management team was careful to clearly articulate to every employee what the sales culture would look like, why it was needed, and the ways in which it would benefit the employees.*
5. Not removing obstacles to the new vision. Hurdles have to be removed, not seen as roadblocks. Someone has to take charge and remove the hurdles. *Roadblocks can sometimes be people who do not embrace the change. If their reticence is not justified, and cannot be corrected, they may need to be removed.*
6. Not systematically planning for and creating short-term "wins." *In the bank's situation we made sure that incentive payouts were on as short a turn-around time as possible in order to reward employees. Whether it is free lunches, t-shirts or prizes, there has to be something to keep people focused and rewarded for the work that has been completed, even before the change effort is completed.*
7. Declaring victory too soon. The change effort has to be completed before victory can be declared. *Sometimes victory does not even need to be declared. Embracing the sales culture for the bank was an ongoing process.*
8. Not anchoring changes in the corporate culture. Communicate the change and then keep communicating. Look for every opportunity to reinforce the change in policies and procedures by way of posters, e-mails, etc. *Every part of the sales program at the bank was made a part of the corporate culture. Change readily becomes a part of the culture when part of the change affects the way a significant portion of the population is compensated.*

The humorous poet Ogden Nash said, "Progress might have been all right once, but it has gone on too long." Change may not always be considered progress but maintaining the status quo is rarely considered progress. As a manager, you frequently have to be a champion for change. Doing this well is good Management Sense for you and your employees.

For your consideration:

a. How do you respond to impending change?
b. What change have you accommodated lately?

## Passive Aggressive Management

Anna is a 61 year old female who reports to Charles, a 52 year old male. Charles does not care for Anna and has a feeling that she does not do a good job although he doesn't know for sure because he never sits down and talks about anything with Anna. Charles really would like for Anna to go away; and in the back of his mind thinks that if he ignores her enough, frustrates and aggravates her enough, she will.

Anna, on the other hand, is trying to do her job; she tries to see Charles and can never get on his schedule. She sends him memos and gets no response. She sends him emails that he ignores. Meetings are held, to which she is not invited, about topics that affect Anna's area. There are decisions made that affect her area about which Charles never consults Anna.

Eventually, Charles comes across someone he would like to have in Anna's job, and he gets serious about getting rid of Anna. He meets with her for the first time in ages to tell her all that he thinks she is doing wrong. He tells her that he is going to have to let her go and will give her a month to find another job.

So what is wrong with this picture?

1. The way in which Charles is treating Anna is immoral, unethical and uncivil.
2. Charles is not doing his job – he is failing to manage a subordinate. A manager manages, rather than ignores, people. This type of management produces an environment that is not as productive as it could be and it is Charles' job to maximize productivity.
3. Charles is sending the message to his other subordinates (Anna's peers) that his behavior toward them and their ultimate success is based on favoritism and other subjective factors rather than an accurate assessment of their performance.
4. Anna will now be able to make the claim that her termination is a violation of Title VII of the Civil Rights Act of 1964 (because of

her gender) and a violation of the Age Discrimination Act of 1967 (while Charles and Anna are both over 40, Anna is significantly older than Charles). That's just the beginning. Anna will also reasonably assert that Charles' behavior toward her (his passive-aggressive style of management) constitutes a hostile work environment, and that will be the proverbial smoking gun for her claim of wrongful termination. This will be a real can of worms for Charles and his employer to try to clean up.

I have seen many managers try to manage people they do not like as I have described Charles' attempt to manage Anna. These managers always think it is a clever and original idea to try to frustrate and aggravate an employee until the employee quits. The manager thinks that in managing this way, they can avoid the HR fundamentals of coaching, counseling and documenting. It is unfortunate and potentially expensive that these managers cannot deal with people in an honest and forthright manner.

Passive aggressive management is not a productive way in which to manage people. We have to utilize good management principles and practices when dealing with our employees. It is not just a matter of complying with the law and avoiding litigation, it is a matter of doing the right thing.

For your consideration:

a. What does "smoking gun" mean?
b. Why do managers try to avoid the HR fundamentals?

## No Sugar-Honey-Ice-Tea; No profanity

Like the previous chapter, this is something you should not do to employees or applicants, but it warrants its own chapter. Do you think profanity in the workplace is harmless, a healthy release, your constitutional right?

First let me break down profanity into two groups: I am not talking about PG profanity here. The words that describe the opposite of heaven or what fish say when they run into a wall are generally not perceived as a problem unless pervasive, directed at a person, or said in front of a guest or customer. Everything else (we'll call it the R-rated profanity): sugar-honey-ice-tea; the f-word; GD; SOB or any combination of these, can be problematic. Most of you wouldn't say these things anyway, but for those who may, please read on.

First there are the old-timey aphorisms: you shouldn't kiss your mama (children, wife, etc.) with that mouth; the use of profanity is an indication of a limited vocabulary. These are good and contain good homespun wisdom.

Then there are the biblical admonitions. Moses brought us what God had to say about using His name in vain, and James has a good comment in James 3:7-10. That's just two of the selections, there is a lot more in scripture on the subject.

Last, but not least, are the implications for the workplace. An employee subjected to hearing the regular use of R-rated profanity could actually file a charge of a hostile environment. Also, when there is a separate charge of harassment and where the use of R-rated profanity was also present, the profanity can be the smoking gun or evidence that management is lax and unprofessional enough to have allowed such things as harassment to go on in the workplace, as evidenced by the R-rated profanity.

Constitutional rights of free speech do not extend to the private sector workplace. Your employer can have a voice in the language you use in the workplace. Standards addressing the use of profanity can and should be set. As managers we have a duty to provide a workplace for our employees that is free of harassment. It is very good Management Sense to clean up your language and the language of your employees if you are a manager.

For your consideration:

a. How can you express urgency, frustration, even anger, without using profanity?
b. What can you do to curb the use of profanity in your workplace?

## Irrational Escalation

In their book *Negotiating Rationally* by Max H. Bazerman and Margaret A. Neale, the authors introduce the concept of "irrational escalation." I would like to co-opt this concept from the world of negotiation and apply it to the world of management.

The authors define irrational escalation as "Continuing a previously selected course of action beyond what rational analysis would recommend."[7] They use it in the context of continuing to pursue a negotiated deal long after the deal ceases to have value. I have seen managers do this in decisions that they make about people.

Let's say a manager has an employee with whom that manager has an investment. The investment could be time, money, loyalty or friendship and frequently is all of these. But the manager receives legitimate feedback from others that this employee is having problems on the job. This feedback is contrary to the manager's bias toward and commitment to the employee, but because of the investment, the manager pursues an irrational course of action with the employee, i.e., continuing to support, promote and reward, while ignoring the feedback that was received regarding the employee.

Further, this positive bias toward the employee is compounded by what Bazerman and Neale call a "confirmation trap."[8] That is, the manager is biased in favor of information that affirms his commitment or decision, and biased against information that is not consistent with that thinking. The manager selectively perceives information that supports his position. Some of the ways that this is done is by discounting the people that provide the feedback, avoiding conflicting sources, seeking only supportive sources and listening only to what is supportive.

Obviously, this is not a good way to make decisions. We must value not only decision making but good decision making. And, as Bazerman and Neale point out, we must value not only good outcomes, but good choices.[9]

Managers must be good decision makers about people by:

1. Consciously deciding not to become involved in irrational escalation. Stop, listen and consider conflicting information. If it has merit, consider it and change your thinking or adjust your plan.
2. Basing the decisions we make on rational information. It does not have to be evidence beyond the shadow of a doubt, but it should be evidence or information that appears, to the reasonable person, to be comprehensive and real.
3. Ensuring that we do not become caught in a confirmation trap, i.e., selecting only information that supports our position while ignoring or not seeking out contradictory information. We must allow and actively seek out balance in the information that affects our decision making. This is why a manager who surrounds himself/herself with people who will only say "yes" is so dangerous; that manager's decision making is inherently one-sided and flawed.

I think one of the worst descriptions of a manager that I hear is when it is said that a manager makes up his or her mind and cannot be budged. That is not an attribute to be proud of – it is a closed mind. Part of developing Management Sense is to maintain an open mind and listen to all input even if it is something you do not want to hear.

For your consideration:

a. Why is it so hard for some managers to change their thinking about an employee?
b. How does a manager avoid being so invested in an employee that the manager cannot see the truth?

# What Judges Think

Some time ago I attended an employment law seminar, and during one of the sessions there were three judges seated on a panel – two federal judges and one magistrate judge. The moderator asked the judges several questions regarding employment law cases over which they had presided. These judges gave pragmatic and highly instructive responses and I would like to share a portion of my notes on the questions and responses:

Moderator's question: Why/when do juries award large punitive damages in employment cases?

Judges' responses:

1. *Because there was direct evidence—the "smoking gun."* For example, this would be the e-mail that refers to an older worker as being over the hill.
2. *When there is a hierarchical difference between plaintiff and offender.* In other words, the plaintiff is a worker and the offender is the manager.
3. *When the jury believes the witness has lied.* Unfortunately, I have observed that lies are present in every lawsuit I have been a part of and I do not think that is unusual. If you lie, you will be caught in that lie eventually.
4. *When there has been an abdication of the management training responsibility by the employer.* Employers have a duty to train managers, to help develop their Management Sense.
5. *When the jurors find themselves asking, "How could they (the employer) have done that?"* A trial gives a jury the opportunity to pull back the curtains and look into the private inner workings of an organization, and sometimes they cannot believe what they see.

Moderator's question: Any general advice on avoiding employment lawsuits?

Judges' responses:

1. *Make employment decisions based on compliance with employment law and what is best for your organization.* This assumes that the managers who are making decisions have some understanding of employment law.
2. *Assume every employment decision you make will be reviewed by eight people from the line at Wal-Mart.* In other words, it is everyday citizens who are going to make up the jury that will be looking at how your managers conducted themselves when dealing with employees.

Do these responses mean we need to make sure we destroy evidence and make sure that we do not get caught lying? Of course not; it means when we make decisions about employees, we make decisions in a consultative manner, considering the specific employee situation within the context of your organization's policies, precedents and culture and in compliance with employment law. And, it means that there is a need for ongoing training for all of those people who are in management positions (such as you), so that they can make good decisions and know when they should consult with HR or senior management on a matter.

For your consideration:

a. Does this mean that we have to make all decisions regarding employees based on what a jury might think?
b. What does the phrase "make decisions in a consultative manner" mean?

## Putting Off Procrastination

My second-grade teacher, Ms. Plant, called me a procrastinator, and I was a victim of this self- fulfilling prophecy for many years. Now I am, proudly, a recovering procrastinator.

Working for several years as an HR consultant where I was not paid until I finished a project helped me get over procrastination. It is much easier to procrastinate at work when someone is paying you regularly, as most employers do, whether you finish anything or not.

To overcome procrastination, learn to identify what defines closure for a task or project and then work toward that goal. Visualize the completed task and then do what needs to be done to get there. Try to finish something worthwhile every day before leaving the workplace.

The task I have observed that is most frequently procrastinated is dealing with poor performance/behavior. Most managers would rather just put up with it, work around it, or play Pass the Lemon, anything but deal directly with the person who is not doing his/her job.

Of course, all of the other employees of this manager realize this; they do not respect the manager; they resent the employee that is getting away with the poor performance and they will eventually lower their performance standards. And why shouldn't they? Other people get away with it.

So that you do not procrastinate in dealing with performance issues:

1. Identify what needs to be done to help the employee with the performance (or behavioral) problem.
2. Visualize how this employee would be performing if he/she were performing adequately and then visualize how you will explain to the employee the gap that exists between his/her performance and what you have visualized.

3. Work with the employee until the employee improves his/her performance or until you determine that there is a mismatch between the job and the employee.

Poor performance or bad behavior on the job can take many forms. It is ultimately the manager's job to identify and then try to modify the undesirable performance or behavior of the employee so that it is in compliance with expectations. In the workplace we typically use verbal coaching or a written warning to communicate to the employee what he/she is doing wrong, what needs to be done to correct the problem, and what will happen if the problem is not corrected.

This seems perfectly rational and logical, so why would a manager procrastinate what is one of the most important elements of the manager's job? Here are some common reasons given by managers:[10]

"I failed to document earlier problems so no record exists on which to base subsequent disciplinary action." *In other words, "I have not done my job before and I am not going to start now." Not issuing the necessary warnings is an insidious affair, but there has to be a start somewhere. Starting late is better than not starting at all.*

"I thought I would get little or no support from higher management for the disciplinary action." *You could be wrong about that, and, even if you are, the action still needs to be taken. In so doing, try to educate upper management or help them grow a backbone. You might also find that higher management is waiting for you to take action.*

"I was uncertain of the facts underlying the situation requiring disciplinary action." *These situations do require some investigation, and that is best done in concert with Human Resources.*

"I did not discipline another employee in the past for a similar infraction and I have to appear consistent." *You cannot refrain from addressing a wrong because the wrong has never before been addressed. It may be that you have to issue a decree stating that from this point on (or by a certain date), anyone who violates this policy, etc., will receive the appropriate disciplinary action.*

"I want to be seen as a likable person." *Most of us do, but sometimes in the course of performing our job, we have to do things at work that someone is not going to like. That is the nature of work.*

It can be painful to deal with people problems, and, initially, it feels good to procrastinate, but, it really does become more painful for you and your other employees the longer you procrastinate in dealing with such problems.

For your consideration:

a. How is a manager's procrastination of dealing with an employee's poor performance viewed by other employees?
b. Can you think of other reasons why managers procrastinate in dealing with matters of poor performance?

## Mis-placed Loyalty

Harry was a very likable fellow but a mediocre salesman, and he did a poor job on his paperwork. The company president received a complaint from a client about Harry's paperwork and then looked at Harry's sales numbers. The president then told Sam, Harry's boss, to get rid of Harry.

Sam had hired Harry, really liked Harry and talked the president into giving Harry some more time. The president went along with Sam's request, even though Sam really had no good defense for Harry's performance. Eight months later, the president had received more complaints and the sales numbers were no better. Again, the president told Sam to terminate Harry's employment. Sam talked to Harry, felt Harry would do a better job and then figured he would just lay low and hoped the president would move on to somebody else.

A month later, the president saw Harry's name on a sales report. He was furious. First he called Harry in and fired him. Then he called Sam in and fired him.

Your loyalty is to your employer, not to your employees.

Are your employees always right? Probably not, if they are human. Should you protect your employees? Not if they are performing/behaving in a manner that is not consistent with the expectations or values of your organization. Do your employees sign your check? I doubt it. It is your employer with whom you are swapping time and expertise for money with the expectation that you will manage people and processes effectively. Therefore, it would seem that you owe more to your employer than to your employees.

Many managers hang on to an employee when the employee is a poor performer, even when they have been advised that the employee should no longer be retained. Why? Here are some reasons:[11]

1. They want to be liked by their employees.
2. They have some kind of personal connection to the employee.
3. They think the employee must be salvageable because they hired him.
4. They hope the problem will disappear.
5. They lack the willingness or ability to confront.
6. They are procrastinators for some or all of the above reasons.

What are the results?

1. Poor productivity – by the offending employee as well as everyone who is aware of the situation
2. Loss of respect for management – employees can see that you are not doing your job and they know that it is your job to manage
3. Poor morale – seeing the offending employee continue uncorrected is a morale downer for everyone involved
4. Turnover – the tension and poor morale created by this kind of situation has an impact on employees' willingness to stay in such an environment
5. Poor use of funds – paying salaries to non-productive employees or giving these employees raises is very poor stewardship

Sam should have followed his president's instructions but he let his mis-placed loyalty to his employee interfere with making a good business decision. A manager's job is to manage and that means getting the right people on the team, communicating expectations, and making corrections if and when necessary.

The other way in which loyalty can be mis-placed is when you, as a manager, expect your employees to be unfailingly loyal to you. Your employee's loyalty should be to the organization, not to you personally.

Loyalty to the organization means that employees support the organization's mission and policies. The organization is what needs to be sustained by support from management and employees so that it is on-going. There is no such need to sustain individuals; individual people come and go during the life of an organization.

When managers require unfailing personal loyalty from employees, there may be some kind of ulterior motive or need. For example:

1. The manager is insecure in his/her position and needs that kind of forced loyalty. Employees see this insecurity and resent the pressure to be loyal to a manager they do not respect.
2. The manager has a narcissistic personality. This is a miserable situation for everyone and the best thing for you to do if you report to this person is find another job. I hate to say that, but you cannot change these people; and if you are miserable, either learn to live with it or move on.
3. The manager has some kind of immoral or illegal motive, and the employee loyalty is necessary to carry on the act. Only the employees with golden handcuffs will put up with this. Everyone else will leave or somehow disassociate themselves from this train wreck.

Hopefully, you do not require your employees to have this kind of personal loyalty to you. If you use your Management Sense and understand the difference between loyalty to you and loyalty to the organization, it won't be a problem for you. Loyalty is a wonderful thing but mis-placed loyalty can be a real problem in the workplace.

For your consideration:

a. What are other reasons managers may be excessively loyal to employees? Is this good or bad?
b. What are your thoughts about the statement, "There is no such need to sustain individuals..."?

# Section 2

# How to Create an Environment in Which Your Employees Will Want to Work

## The Poetry of Retention

I would define retention as keeping those employees that you want to keep. And if you do not want to keep all that you have, I would expect that you are working to manage out the door (OTD) those that you do not want to keep. Anyway…

I believe that an employee's immediate manager may have a more direct effect on the retention of employees than any other factor. It is not pay, benefits or how close to the front door your parking place is. It is the manager and how he treats his employees. Think about it – probably your best work situation had to do with the fact that you reported to a great manager.

Anecdotally, that is what I hear consistently: People will put up with a lot, as far as poor pay, etc., to work for someone they really respect and like, but not vice versa. Or, as I have said before, people will work longer and harder for good management and poor pay than they will for poor management and good pay.

After interviewing over 80,000 employees, Gallup pollsters Buckingham and Coffman came to the same conclusion, "people leave managers, not companies."[12] They confirmed that, in the end, if you have a turnover problem in your company, you probably have a manager problem.

I was so inspired over this subject that I was moved to write the following verse describing how a manager can affect an otherwise contented employee:

*My Reason for Leaving*

By Fred Rogan

*I love my work, it makes me feel fine.*
*I love my co-workers; we have a good time.*
*Our customers are great, the best folks on earth.*
*I enjoy all these people, they fill me with mirth.*
*The salary they pay me is a little low,*
*But the benefits I love, we have PTO.*
*My workspace is fine, if just a bit small,*
*And one of my best friends works just down the hall.*
*But I'm thinking of leaving, getting out of this work,*
*'Cause wouldn't you know it: My boss is a jerk.*

Why is it so important that you try to have a positive impact on retaining your employees?

1. Turnover costs money. There are the direct costs of replacing the employee: ads, interviewing and overtime incurred. And there are the indirect costs of customer inconveniences or lost productivity due to staffing shortages. It adds up.
2. When you lose people, you lose human capital. Human capital is the knowledge of an organization (its history, how things work, how things get done, etc.) that an employee has as well as the knowledge, skills and abilities that enables an employee to do the job. All of this knowledge belongs to the employee. An employee owns her own human capital, and when she leaves, she takes her human capital with her. You have to calculate the loss of that human capital when you lose an employee because it will have to be replaced.
3. Your team building is negatively affected by turnover. You cannot build a great team unless you can keep a team together. People have to be together and go through the team development that it takes to work together and be effective. If the team members are always changing, you are not going to have the team development that is necessary.

Retention is important, and, as a manager, you have a very large role in the retention of employees. You are the one with whom your employees interact on a daily basis, you are the one that they look to for guidance, and you are the one who contributes most to creating an environment in which employees will want to work. Most of this book is about how you can favorably affect retention and not be the horse's rear end that makes people want to work elsewhere. Take seriously not being a horse's rear end by using your Management Sense and being the best manager you can be.

For your consideration:

a. Do you agree or disagree with the theory that managers have a major impact on retention? Why?
b. Why is it your job as a manager to manage human capital?

## Issuing Good Instructions to Employees

Billy had already had a bad day by the time he arrived at work. He and his wife had had a fight, and his children were horrible in the car as he dropped them off at day care. Then Billy came into the office and found that all of the reports prepared for his big meeting had errors. The first person he saw was his administrative assistant, Susan.

"HOW IN THE #&@* DID THIS HAPPEN?" Billy demanded, veins bulging. "DO I NOT PAY YOU ENOUGH TO GET ANYTHING DONE CORRECTLY?!?! THE MEETING IS ONLY TWO HOURS AWAY – THERE IS NO WAY WE CAN BE READY!!"

There was a small crisis here and Billy did not handle it well. Susan may get the reports ready for the meeting, but her relationship with Billy will be damaged because of the way in which he was delivering the message. To the detriment of Billy, Susan will most likely withdraw from him after this episode, and Billy will either have to apologize for his behavior, or there will be a long recovery period. This is not really the most productive use of time or best environment in which to work, especially if Billy's reaction is a pattern.

How managers speak to employees largely determines how well employees regard that manager (it is the most obvious thing to go on) as well as how things get done. Here are some things to remember when giving instructions to employees:

1. Don't talk down to your employees – They know you are the boss, don't rub it in. What is talking down? Speaking to them as if they were a child; using an aggravated tone of voice, wagging your finger or some other display of anger. Being talked down to is a frequent complaint made by employees and can be construed to be racist or sexist.
2. Use appropriate tone and wording – Try speaking to your employees with the same courtesy/tone/wording that you use with your boss. Instructions given to anyone should be given as a polite request. Just

because people work for you doesn't mean you should use words and a tone of voice with them that sounds as if you are in the military (unless you are in the military).
3. Be precise – Make sure you clearly state what is expected and give guidelines on quality and quantity of performance and on deadlines. Two common errors are failure to state a deadline and expecting the employee to be able to read your mind. Take your time, think through what you really need, give accurate instructions, and the assignment is likely to be completed right the first time.
4. Think about to whom you are talking – Does this employee have the ability, experience and motivation to do what you are asking? Setting an employee up for failure is not in the best interest of that person or the organization that you serve.
5. Be clear – Make certain that the employee understands you by clearly stating what it is that you want the employee to do as well as asking the employee for feedback to be sure your message was received.

You cannot give good instructions to employees if you are angry or upset. Giving good instructions means your employees hear, understand and are willing to follow up on what you want them to do and the way you want them to do it.

Make sure that your message is not mangled by the manner in which you deliver it. The point of communication is to convey a message. If you are angry or upset, you need to wait until you are sure that your emotions are in check and that your Management Sense is in control.

For your consideration:

a. How does the presence of a strong emotion such as anger make instructions less clear?
b. What can you do to ensure that emotions do not interfere with the giving of instructions?

# Clear Communication

Clear communication is when the lines of communication are open in both directions, up and down, back and forth; it is when reception is equivalent in quality to transmission. Here are some suggestions for communicating more clearly:

1. Employees like to know what is going on with their employer, rather than being kept in the dark. Unless it is confidential, share information with employees. Let employees be plugged in. Unless it has to do with proprietary information or employee privacy, be transparent.
2. Think before you speak. How many times in personal conversations do we wish we could take back something that we said? It is even more critical in the employment setting that you engage your brain before speaking. How is what you say to an employee going to sound when you hear it repeated back to you by a plaintiff's attorney?
3. Remember that you are communicating with adults. No one in the workplace likes to be spoken to as if he/she is a child.
4. Be a good listener. Listen for the point the speaker is trying to make and do not jump to the point you think they are trying to make. Good, active listening is difficult for us to do; it takes practice and concentration, but there is no more important place for this to occur than in the workplace (with those people above and below your position). And, you really cannot actively listen while you are doing something else.
5. Be conscious of your non-verbal communication. You sometimes say a lot without saying anything (rolling your eyes, yawning, a sigh, a grimace). Most non-verbal communication is as readily understood as the words we use, so be careful what you say non-verbally.
6. The manner is as important as the message. If you communicate in anger, frustration, etc., that manner is going to confuse the message so badly that you should have no expectation of your real message being understood or acted upon, thus making you look somewhat silly.

You cannot communicate in any way that you please while on the job. Your communication must be at a level and in a manner that is different from your communication outside of work. More importantly, because we are dependent on the support of others to do our jobs, we must communicate in ways that are going to be perceived as good, open communication.

For your consideration:

a. How do we ensure that we are clearly communicating with those whom we manage?
b. Why can't you, as a manager, communicate in any manner you choose while at work?

## Orientation to Departmental Orientation

It was not all that unusual to receive an EEOC complaint while I was in banking – it was a large bank. What was unusual was a complaint in which an employee said that he was terminated because of his religion: Baptist. You don't see that every day.

The employee, Rodney, alleged in his complaint that he was required to come in on the weekend and, therefore, could not rehearse in his church's praise band, which rehearsed on Saturday for Sunday services. Rodney alleged that we had not made a reasonable accommodation for his religion.

As part of my investigation of the complaint, I went to the mailroom at our operations center, where Rodney had worked, and asked about scheduling. The mailroom required each employee to work either a Saturday or a Sunday, one time per month, the employee's choice. In addition, I discovered, employees that worked on Sunday did not have to come in until after church services if they chose to attend.

I also was shown a sheet that was given to all employees before being hired explaining all of this and saw the same sheet with Rodney's signature, acknowledging that he had been informed of the work requirements BEFORE he was even hired.

I complimented the mailroom manager for his thoroughness, went back to my office and wrote a response to the EEOC. The complaint was dropped.

Orienting employees well is not just about prevailing on EEOC complaints, but if that is a by-product, it is a good one. When you hire a new employee in your area, one of the most important things is to ensure that he/she gets a good start. The best way to do this is to follow a checklist:

1. Introductions
    a. Introduce the new employee to every person in the department. Explain each person's role.

b. Pair the new employee up with a buddy (preferably his/her co-worker or trainer) for lunch, tours, etc.
   c. Show the physical layout of both the department (water, restrooms, coffee, copier) and the building/grounds (security, break room, parking, etc.).
2. Training
   a. Show the employee his job goals/description.
   b. Let the employee know how she will be evaluated.
   c. Tell and show the employee what he will do.
   d. Explain how the employee's job fits into the big picture.
   e. Let the employee know who will train her.
   f. Explain how long training will last.
   g. Train the employee (more in the chapter "Steps to Employee Training").
3. Expectations (recommended to be put in writing)
   a. Performance – tell him what is expected
   b. Behavior – tell her what is expected
   c. Dress code – tell him what is expected
4. Conditions of employment (recommended to be put in writing)
   a. Starting and quitting times
   b. Lunch: when and how long
   c. How much, if any, overtime may be required
   d. How vacations are requested
   e. Who is to be notified and by what time if the employee is sick
   f. Office procedures/e-mail
   g. Telephone rules and operation
5. Chain of command
   a. Department organization
   b. Who is in charge? Who is next in charge?

A new employee is a significant investment, and you need to make sure that you do all that you can to get the new employee off to a good, positive start. Follow this outline to orient the employee, and then be sure to follow up in four to six weeks to make sure the employee is really becoming a part of the team. Expectations and conditions of employment should be shared with final applicants just like the mailroom manager did with Rodney.

For your consideration:

a. How many of these items do you have as a part of your orientation process for new employees?
b. What is the most important outcome of orienting new employees well?

## Promoting a Training Culture

One of the hospitals I worked for was a for-profit hospital. After the mid-year budget assessment every year, we would have some kind of downsizing. And, every year the department that was downsized first and cut most severely was the training department. In many organizations, the first thing cut or the last thing implemented is a training function.

This is kind of strange when you think about it since most organizations want their employees to know certain things and act certain ways. The training function is one of the few areas charged with ensuring that employees have a standard level of knowledge or skills related to their jobs and the mission of the organization.

If your organization does not have a training function that engenders a training culture (and perhaps even if it does) here are some things you can do now for the training and development of your employees:

1. Coach – provide a flow of comments and suggestions to your employees. Managing their performance (a part of your job) will naturally entail a lot of training and development.
2. Cross-train – it is good for your department and good for your organization to have redundancy in as many positions as possible. An employee's absence from the job should rarely mean that work/service has to go undone. Being cross trained in other jobs is an enriching experience for employees.
3. Initiate job rotation – allow employees to briefly work in different areas within your department to give them a better perspective on how jobs fit together. This will also give them a new perspective on their own job.
4. Assign special projects – giving employees a special project can be enriching. This should not be filing the two years' worth of paperwork in your office, but a project in which the employee can stretch out and learn while doing meaningful work.

5. Hold staff meetings – believe it or not these can be enriching to employees. Not the "what have you done since we last met" kind, but rather the "what problems or issues need to be solved/addressed and who has ideas?" kind. Provide your employees the opportunity to create synergy.
6. Share your knowledge – you must know something to have gotten to the position you now hold. Share it. Frequently managers think that sharing knowledge weakens them or makes them vulnerable when, actually, sharing knowledge strengthens managers by making them developers of people and purveyors of power (as in "knowledge is power").

Training and developing your employees is a big part of being a selfless, employee-centered coach. Most of these actions listed above can be completed with no training budget and no training department. It is good Management Sense to train your employees and to create a training culture.

For your consideration:

a. What kinds of knowledge and skills does your organization expect employees to possess?
b. How are employees expected to obtain your organization's expected level of knowledge and skills?

## Steps to Employee Training

Reading exit interviews over the years, I would say that one of the most consistent comments by employees is that they felt that the training that they received for their jobs was inadequate. Based on what I have read in exit interviews, it really seems to aggravate people that they are hired and then not trained or not trained well to do a job. When people are first hired, they have an expectation that they will be shown how to do a job, and they have a readiness to be trained that is unique to the new employee. You need to take advantage of this receptiveness to training of newly hired (or newly promoted) employees and give them a good start on their new job.

With the goal of your organization to have well-trained employees, I offer the following practical methods to guide you in instructing a new employee or a current employee on a new job or a new skill:

Before you can train you must:
1. Prioritize what the employee must know. Have a plan.
2. Have the workplace properly arranged, just as the employee will need it to be.

Then, train according to the following steps:

Step One – Prepare the employee
1. Create an environment that is conducive to learning.
2. Find out what the employee already knows about the job.
3. Give the employee a big-picture view of the job.

Step Two – Present the job duties and knowledge that are required
1. Tell, show, illustrate and question in order to convey the new knowledge and operations.
2. Instruct slowly, clearly, completely and patiently, one point at a time.
3. Check and question what the employee knows.

4. Make sure the employee really knows what to do.
5. Put the process/procedure in writing for the employee.

Step Three – Performance tryout
1. Check the employee by having her perform the job.
2. Ask questions about what the employee is doing beginning with why, how, when or where.
3. Observe performance, correct errors and repeat instructions if necessary.
4. Continue until you are certain the employee knows.

Step Four – Follow up
1. Let the employee work alone.
2. Check frequently to be sure the employee is performing adequately.
3. Taper off extra supervision until the employee is qualified to work with normal supervision.

Remember: This person is new on the job; if you want him to know how to do the job, then you have to do some training. If you do not train an employee to do the job the way you want the employee to do it, then the employee will do however it is easiest, quickest, etc., but not necessarily how you want it done. You must invest some time in the above steps with the employee to do effective training and the results will be worth the time and effort.

For your consideration:

a. Describe the best job training that you have ever received.
b. What happens when new employees do not receive the training they need and expect?

## Employees Expect Expectations

Whenever I do performance appraisal training, I always ask, "Would it be fair to appraise an employee without advising the employee beforehand of the basis of the appraisal?" The unison answer is always "NO." Yet, appraising employees without communicating expectations is what the majority of managers do.

What are expectations? They are the manner in which you expect an employee to perform and to behave on the job. Let's not forget about behavior: I have had to terminate the employment of far more people over the years for behavior than for performance. You may call them performance expectations or performance standards; it does not matter what you call them as long as you communicate them.

Expectations can also be the basis of the performance appraisal. An employee has to understand what is expected before she can do the job. It is just that simple.

You or someone in your organization should write the performance expectations. Expectations should be locally owned and operated, and they should support your strategic plan. (If you do not know what your strategic plan is, find out.)

How do you write expectations about performance? You address:

1. Meeting deadlines
2. Quantity expectations
3. Quality expectations
4. Customer service expectations

How do you write expectations about behavior? You address:

1. Punctuality
2. How an employee dresses
3. How an employee interacts with customers, co-workers, vendors

4. An employee's speech, what they say and how they say it. Free speech rights do not extend to the workplace unless you are working for the government.

Your organization may have policies that address most of the above. If you want to add to or elaborate, be sure to check with your HR department.

When do you communicate expectations?

1. As soon as you can after you are promoted to a management position
2. When you start a new job in a management position
3. At the beginning of the fiscal or calendar year
4. When a new employee starts or is promoted into your department

Employees do not like working in the dark, literally or figuratively. When employees do not have the benefit of knowing what is expected of them, you are making them work in the dark. It is good Management Sense to tell employees what is expected of them.

For your consideration:

a. What are you currently telling employees regarding what behavior and performance levels are expected of them?
b. Can you think of times other than those mentioned above to communicate expectations?

## Management Terrorism

Once upon a time, there was a company where the CEO had a longtime friend named Pete. Pete and the CEO had grown up together playing in garage bands back in the '60s and decades later the CEO asked Pete to join the oldies band that the CEO had started just for fun. The band played rock-and-roll oldies, and they were pretty good. During the period that Pete played in the band, Pete was the only member of the five-piece band that did not work for his friend, the CEO.

There was no question that Pete's friend thought he was CEO of the band as well as the company. That was not how Pete saw it. To Pete, being in the band was for fun, and since Pete did not work for the CEO, he would express his opinion freely. Whether it was the chords to a song, how they arranged a song or what gigs they played, Pete felt comfortable taking issue with the CEO. Not that he always did, but if there was a position that Pete felt needed to be expressed, he had no qualms about expressing it. The CEO couldn't fire Pete from his day job since he did not work for him, and Pete did not think the CEO would kick him out of the band.

The other guys in the band that worked for the CEO at their real jobs were not as lucky as Pete. They did not ever disagree with the CEO because he was what some people might describe as a screamer, an intimidator or a bully. The other guys wouldn't take issue with the CEO over the band issues, much less their real job issues as they knew they would incur his wrath. They were victims of management terrorism.

Terrorism is the use of fear as a means of coercion. Management terrorism is when a manager uses fear in order to get people to do what the manager wants them to do. The manager creates fear in the employee by using threats, expressed or implied. The threats are of losing a job, losing a bonus, losing status or losing a way of life. The other guys that played in the band were paid very well for their day jobs, and they did not want to jeopardize those jobs by arguing about something as insignificant as issues in a rock-and-roll band. The fear that was evident in that band was real.

When people are threatened or afraid, it affects their biology. They have negative reactions:[13]

1. They avoid the person making the threats.
2. They withdraw.
3. They may become depressed because of what they perceive as the lack of control of their lives.
4. Their bodies have chemical reactions that cause stress that in turn affects critical thinking, creativity and memory.

Nothing good comes from using terrorism to manage employees. Good managers are able to select the right people, train them effectively, and then delegate responsibly so that the work is done in a way that provides the greatest benefit to the organization. Granted, creating fear in employees to get them to do their job may work for a short period of time. However, the negative side effects more than outweigh any short-term benefits. Managers who use management terrorism to manage employees do so because they have a very limited understanding of Management Sense. Managers like that will not be effective for long and will create significant negative unintended consequences.

For your consideration:

a. Describe a time when a manager should use fear to motivate.
b. How does a manager who uses fear to motivate then reverse course?

## Just Kidding, Not Really

Phil liked for his administrative assistant, Sherry (a very good employee) to have his coffee ready for him as soon as he got into the office. One day he came in and there was no coffee and no Sherry. She was apparently late, but came in after about 15 minutes and brought his coffee.

"I ought to fire you for being late and not having the coffee ready when I got here," he said. Sherry looked at him, feeling hurt and surprised, and said, "There was so much traffic; there must have been a wreck. I'm sorry I was late."

Phil responded, "That's OK, you know I wouldn't really fire you for that. I was just kidding."

Phil's behavior is not appropriate for a manager. Not just because he doesn't get his own coffee but also because:

1. You never, ever say, "I *ought* to fire you…" to an employee. If the employee needs to be fired, do it, but do not make such a threat unless you are sitting down in a formal counseling session and are telling the employee that her job is in jeopardy, and there are legitimate, non-discriminatory reasons to support that. Threatening a person's job is serious business to that person and not the way to motivate people.
2. Sherry doesn't know Phil wouldn't fire her for being late. He just said he would and he is her boss. She can only go by what he says. If he says things like that and does not follow through, when can she believe him?
3. The words "I was just kidding" should never be used in the context of anything to do with an employee's job. Employees just do not like to have their manager kidding around about their job, their income, their future.

I have frequently encountered managers who like to say what they really think, even though it may be unsupportable or inappropriate, and then try to cover up by using sarcasm or saying, "I was just kidding." It doesn't work. In a legal setting such as a deposition, when a manager is under oath and has to affirm having made such a statement to an employee, the statement will appear incredibly immature.

It may be pop-psychology, but it is pretty accurate pop-psychology to say that there is always some truth in kidding. If there is a problem with an employee, then you need to rationally think about the employee's behavior that is bothering you and make a decision as to whether it rises to the level of something that needs to be addressed. If it does, deal with it as a manager; if it doesn't, let it go.

When you are communicating with employees, you cannot kid about the terms and conditions of their employment. You must also not kid about race, age, gender, religion, national origin or any other protected factor. Kidding with employees about work-related matters is something you must grow out of, and I am not kidding.

For your consideration:

a. Why do you think managers use sarcasm or kidding when dealing with employees?
b. What problems could the inappropriate use of sarcasm or kidding with employees cause?

## PITA People

Pain in the a-- people. They are everywhere. One of the worst that I have ever had to help a manager deal with was an administrative assistant I'll call Mildred. Mildred had the department head completely fooled, and the things she did behind his back – exceeding her authority, misusing his authority and just being mean to everyone – were tearing the department apart.

The department managers first approached me saying they were all on the verge of quitting but they also feared for the department head's success because they actually thought Mildred was capable of completely undermining him. Finally, after the managers provided evidence, I was able to convince the department head that he had a problem with Mildred. Then, after a year or so of trying to no avail to change her behavior, we were able to assist Mildred's departure from the organization. There was concern because Mildred was in two protected classes (over 40 years of age and a female), but she took no action against the organization after her termination, and I think we would have been prepared had she done so.

Here are some suggestions for dealing with difficult people[14]:

1. Do not label PITA people as PITA people no matter how bad they are (sounds like a Catch 22, doesn't it?). Labeling them is a conclusion and is not a good place to start.
2. Think in terms of behaviors, not PITA people. We did try to specifically point out behaviors to Mildred so that she could change.
3. The easiest way to cope with some people is to avoid them, but the easiest answer isn't always the best answer. Change your mindset and focus on what they do well. Accentuate the positive. Some people like Mildred you cannot avoid even if you want to because they draw such attention to themselves.
4. Take control of the situation, use his or her name and make eye contact. This was effective with Mildred one on one.

5. Talk with them in private; give them your undivided attention – an absolute part of due process.
6. Avoid accusations; ask open-ended questions and listen to his or her side of the story. Mildred had her own version of things that we had to check out.
7. Clearly state that you expect the behavior to improve. We told Mildred what she was doing wrong, and what she needed to do to fix it. We focused on the behaviors.
8. Establish deadlines and timetables for the behavior to cease.
9. Discuss the long-term rewards for positive behaviors and the consequences of not improving.
10. Enforce the consequences of failure to improve.
11. If the behavior does not change, consider asking for assistance from Human Resources. The affected department did and eventually we resolved the matter although it meant Mildred leaving. Not every person is willing or able to change his or her behavior, and then you have to take the necessary action to take them off the team.

Unfortunately, Mildred chose to not change her behavior; perhaps she did not know how. We may not always be able to change difficult people but we can manage them or manage them out the door. PITA people cannot be allowed to disrupt the workplace. The next chapter provides greater detail for dealing with bad behavior on the job.

For your consideration:

a. What are the consequences of not dealing with PITA people?
b. What are the consequences of dealing with PITA people?

## Bad Attitudes

I wish I had $100 for every time I have heard managers say, "I have an employee who does a good job but has a bad attitude; what do I do?" I would be richer than a plaintiff's attorney.

Latisha, a bank branch manager, called me and said that her Customer Service Representative, Erma, was being rude to customers and employees, and just generally had a bad attitude. I asked Latisha what exactly Erma was doing. Erma, she said, was not replying to people when they spoke to her, her speaking style was curt and short, and she would roll her eyes when she became the least bit frustrated. Those are behaviors we can address specifically, and ones we can work on improving.

Telling someone they have a bad attitude is just picking a fight. Latisha came to the conclusion that Erma has a bad attitude because of Erma's behaviors. But it is the behaviors that need to be addressed, not the conclusion. So what do you do?

Here are some thoughts:

1. Do not tell the employee he/she has a bad attitude. That is not helpful. To tell someone that they have a bad attitude does not specify the behavior that you wish to extinguish and usually angers the employee.
2. Talk to the employee about the behaviors. If the employee is rude, abrupt, doesn't speak or speaks curtly, etc., those are behaviors that can be used as specific examples to coach or counsel the employee.
3. You must take some action. If you do nothing to deal with the employee's behavior, it will make you look ineffective to others you supervise, not to mention the negative impact it will have on those who come in contact with the employee.
4. Here's what you can do:
    a. Make talking points of the employee's specific behaviors.
    b. Set up a meeting with the employee.

c. Share your observations with the employee.
d. Try to stay as non-confrontational as possible at this point.
e. Ask the employee for his/her thoughts on how the situation can be improved.
f. Set up a mutually agreed upon action plan on how to change these behaviors.
g. Be supportive and positive that the employee can change the behaviors.
h. Follow up if the behavior is not changed.
i. Rehearse future scenarios and what options the employee may have for responding
j. Document all of the above.

Far more employees have trouble on the job for behavioral issues than performance/competence issues. It is a more difficult problem for managers to address, but you must address these matters for the good of all of your employees and to demonstrate that you have good Management Sense.

For your consideration:

a. What do you think people mean when they say an employee has a bad attitude?
b. In thinking of an employee with a "bad attitude" what behaviors led you to that conclusion?

## Dysfunctional Self-Selection Cycle

"Dysfunctional Self-Selection Cycle" is an impressive term that I learned many years ago at a compensation seminar held by what was known then as the American Society for Personnel Administration. The term means that unless you manage compensation properly, the eagles will soar and the turkeys will stay.

The cycle refers to the annual cycle of salary increases in which many organizations engage. The self-selection part means that people will select themselves to leave if they feel they are not being compensated properly. And the dysfunctional part comes in because this process, as described, is detrimental to the operation of any organization.

Let's say I manage a group of five employees. Marie is my poorest performer and is also somewhat volatile. She is a door slammer, has been known to scream at people and very easily becomes emotional. In doing performance appraisals, I give Marie the same score as that of my other employees, and she therefore receives a comparable raise. Word gets out about this, and I am viewed correctly as spineless. My two best employees transfer out of the department because they feel they should have received better raises with Marie receiving less. The remaining employees decide that they can do less and get by because of how I rewarded Marie for her poor performance and behavior. This is the dysfunctional self-selection cycle in action.

How do you avoid the dysfunctional self-selection cycle?

*Recognize good performance* – The best performers should get the best increases. Employees tend to know what their co-workers receive. If Alice Accomplish sees Marie Mediocre (both of whom live up to their name) receive a raise equal to or greater than hers, she will self-select, and it may well be dysfunctional if she leaves. If Alice knows that she gets no recognition for her hard work and, even worse, that Marie gets by with doing nothing day in and day out, the matter is compounded in her eyes.

*Recognize poor performance; this must be done in compensation and in word (written and verbal).* Marie must receive a smaller raise (or no raise at all) than Alice. You do not have to tell Alice; she will know. It is absolutely necessary that you are able to back up this lower raise for Marie with some kind of documentation. If Alice knows you are sincerely working with Marie (again, she will know) to improve her performance or to give her the opportunity to explore other career options, she will know that you distinguish between her performance and Marie's.

Failing to recognize the cause and effect of the dysfunctional self-selection cycle can cause retention problems, productivity problems and morale problems. Using your Management Sense, you can avoid getting caught up in this very negative cycle.

For your consideration:

a. Why do you need to be able to back-up or defend the lower raise for Marie?
b. Can't you do something about Alice and Marie discussing salaries?

## Harassment – Don't Do It or Allow It

The bank I worked with had a local branch that was one of many that were predominantly female. This one local branch also had a male branch manager and a male guard. Every day, some of the females and the male guard would eat lunch in the break room and would have the television tuned to their favorite soap operas while they ate.

If you have ever watched soap operas on daytime television, you know that there is a lot of sexual content on these shows. Familiarity and the shared experience of watching these shows together meant that a great deal of talk centered on sex. The male guard became too comfortable with his female co-workers, and one day, on his way out of the break room, he grabbed a female co-worker's bottom.

Obviously, the guard was seriously out of line. He committed a serious offense by touching a female co-worker where he should not have touched her. But, the branch manager was also at fault. The branch manager knew the group watched the soap operas every day, and he was aware of the sexual banter that ensued. He was at fault because he did not step in as the party-pooper, remind these people that they were at work and put the news on the television.

It is your job as a manager to act as the party-pooper on occasion. You, as the manager in your area, have the front-line responsibility. What does this mean for you?

1. Enforce a zero tolerance policy – this does not mean you fire anyone who commits the smallest infraction, but it does mean that even the smallest infraction is addressed in an appropriate manner. You must actively enforce the zero tolerance policy, meaning if you see a wrong, you must seek to make it right, even if you are not called upon to do so.

2. Know what constitutes (sexual) harassment – this term includes, but is not limited to, offensive language, jokes or other verbal, graphic or physi-

cal conduct relating to an employee's race, sex, religion, color, national origin, age, disability or other factor protected by law that would make the reasonable person experiencing such harassment uncomfortable in the work environment or that could interfere with the person's job performance.

3. Know how to respond to complaints – never tell an employee to "forget it," "don't let it bother you," etc. Say nothing that would sound as if you are discounting the complaint or the complainant. Also, you cannot agree to keep the complaint to yourself – let the complainant know this if such a request is made.

4. Protect the complainant against retaliation. Retaliation is serious and can expose your organization to significant liability. Any hint of retaliation must be dealt with promptly and decisively.

5. Do not require the complainant to put the complaint in writing. Requiring this can have a chilling effect on the filing of complaints or can be perceived as placing a hurdle in the way of a complainant. If the complainant prefers not to submit a written report, get HR or some other senior management, neutral, third party to conduct an interview and make notes of the allegations.

6. Never make changes in the complainant's or the alleged harasser's employment situation before contacting HR or senior management.

7. Contact HR or senior management as soon as possible if there is a report of harassment in any form.

Racial harassment, sexual harassment or harassment of any kind, including bullying, has no place at your organization. It is incumbent upon everyone in a management position to see that it does not occur.

For your consideration:

a. Do you know what employment law is the basis for the prohibition against harassment?
b. What makes it difficult for a manager to be the "party pooper"?

## Retaliation – Don't Do It or Allow It Either

Liz was a manager who supervised about 10 people. For some reason, Liz thought it was okay to come in late, leave early, especially on Fridays, and just generally not do much work. One of Liz's employees reported this to me. I conducted an investigation and confirmed that what the employee told me about Liz's work habits was in fact true. When Liz's boss and I confronted Liz to correct this behavior, one of the first things Liz wanted to know was which one of her employees had told me.

For some reason, I did not think that Liz wanted to bake this employee a cake. What Liz had in mind, was some form of retaliation.

I would define retaliation as taking some action to get back at someone for some real or perceived injury. Retaliation in the workplace is very bad business. Some managers think that they can retaliate in a very subtle manner and since no one is as smart as they are, no one will catch it. Absolutely not true. The recipient of the retaliation will recognize it for what it is, as will anyone who observes the behavior.

Retaliation at work is behavior that is petty, small, bad-mannered, and most likely illegal. It becomes especially serious when retaliatory behavior can be connected to any charge of discrimination, any use of leave protected by the Family Medical Leave Act (FMLA), or any on the job injury. In other words, if an employee exercises any of her statutory rights and then feels that she has been retaliated against for doing so, bingo! Lawsuit amended or new lawsuit initiated.

Retaliation is very negative behavior, and if you think about it, it is very much like the behavior of a four year old. Use your grown-up Management Sense instead and do not ever engage in any kind of retaliatory behavior or let any employee engage in retaliatory behavior.

For your consideration:

a. Are you required to tell an accused employee who his/her accuser is?
b. What effect would unchecked retaliation have in the workplace?

## Things You Should Never Say or Do to an Employee (or Applicant):

How you speak to your employees is an area where you really cannot just use your common sense – you must use Management Sense. As a manager, director or vice president, what you say (it doesn't have to be in writing) or do to employees can be binding or have a significant impact on your organization. You must have and you must use Management Sense. Here are 10 things that you, as a manager, with the power and authority that has been vested in you by your employer, must not say or do:

1. Do not say to a person that he/she has a job as long as he/she wants. This creates an implied contract and it is binding. Many of you work in an employment-at-will state and for an employment-at-will employer; you do not want to do anything that jeopardizes that status.
2. Do not talk to one of your employees about any other of your employees. Talk to your boss or talk to someone in HR, but do not discuss any of your employees with their peers. This mistake is most frequently made with a manager talking out of turn with his/her secretary. A secretary is not a member of management and does not have a need to know and should not be your soul mate.
3. Do not make a promise before you have approval. Do not promise a raise, a promotion, a salary for a new hire or any other significant employment action until you first have all of the appropriate approvals to take such an action.
4. Do not make an exception to a stated policy. Unless you have approval from senior management, you may be exposing your organization to significant liability. Know what your policies are and abide by them. Yes, you are special, but you still have to follow the rules.
5. Do not tell an employee that you are speaking "off the record." There is no such thing. By making such a comment, what you are really saying to the employee is, "Listen closely, I am about to say something foolish."
6. Do not create close friendships with those whom you supervise. That

is a difficult thing to say and do. But if you have a close friendship with a person you supervise, it will impair your ability to be objective about that person and it will impair your ability to take the very actions that define your manager/employee relationship. Such a friendship can also be the basis of a charge of favoritism and, subsequently, discrimination by other employees.
7. Do not hit or kick an employee or hit or kick a piece of furniture that is in close proximity to the employee. First of all, if you are having this kind of anger management problem, we need to get you some counseling, medication or both. Second, doing this could land you and/or your employer in state court on assault charges.
8. Do not prevent an employee from leaving your office or a particular area. You may, for instance, tell an employee that they are required to finish a job or require him/her to work overtime. You may not physically intervene if that employee chooses to leave. The employee may be disciplined for insubordination, but you do not want to be tried in state court for false imprisonment.
9. Do not tell jokes at an employee's expense. Humor in the workplace is a good thing, but making an employee the butt of your jokes can backfire in the form of your jokes' being made the basis of a hostile environment charge.
10. Do not ask an employee, "When are you going to retire?" This statement can be used against you as evidence of age discrimination. It is always best to let the employee bring up the issue of retirement.

Keep in mind that the power and authority given to managers at various levels is based upon the level at which you operate and the discretion of executive management to grant such power and authority. However, it is my understanding that the courts have consistently maintained that it is the employer's duty to ensure that managers act only within the power and authority granted by the employer, and the employer may be held responsible, even if the manager goes beyond the power and authority granted. Don't make your employer sorry they gave you the power and authority of a manager.

For your consideration:

a. How does your employer vest power and authority in you as a manager?
b. Doesn't putting things in writing limit your options as a manager?

# Evaluating Employee Performance

When I was managing all of the EEOC complaints and employment lawsuits for the bank where I worked, I began to see a trend. Performance appraisals were more of a liability than an asset to the bank. In other words, in trying to defend the bank, I was finding on a regular basis that the performance appraisals of the employees terminated were not consistent with the action taken by the bank. Or, the performance appraisals were so vague as to be neither a help nor a hindrance.

Part of the problem was the performance appraisal itself. It was a one-size-fits-all type, and there was no training and no instructions on how to use the form. It was trait-based (initiative, dependability, etc.) and was not taken seriously by managers. Yet, it was used as the basis for administrative decisions including raises.

When performance appraisals are used for administrative purposes (raises, promotions, reductions in force), they must be defensible. When an employee questions an administrative decision that was based on a performance appraisal, you will want to be able to show:

1. That you were comparing the employee's performance to some performance criteria;
2. That you used a standardized method to score the appraisal;
3. That the appraisal was job related;
4. That the appraisal was not vague or subjective;
5. That you can back up your conclusion on the appraisal with job-related evidence.

A paper I read recently addressed the issue of how to evaluate employee performance without creating legal liability. This is a very critical aspect of this process, so here is a synopsis of that paper in which the authors offer these suggestions:[15]

1. Be brutally honest and accurate. Performance appraisals are not the time or place to be nice, to be forgiving or to do subordinates a favor. Nothing can lead to liability faster than performance appraisals that are inconsistent with performance. They must be accurate. Admittedly, this is hard to do, especially when you are telling an employee that some of her performance may be substandard. Some of the following points will help.

2. Keep it job related. While an employee may be a good person that is not what the performance appraisal is about. It is about how well the employee met job-related expectations and how he conducted himself on the job. This does imply that you have communicated job expectations to the employee.

3. Keep it objective and strive to avoid personal opinion. Phrases like "not a team player" or "bad attitude" are subjective, personal opinion statements – do not use them. However, saying "does not share information with peers" and "refuses to speak when spoken to" are more objective and informative to the employee. Pure opinions unsupported by facts have the potential for hiding unfairness or subconscious discrimination. In addition, vagueness deprives the employee of a fair chance to improve.

4. Be consistent relative to other employees in the group. If employees are in the same or similar jobs, be sure to apply the same performance criteria to all of these employees. Do not compare employees to one another but to performance criteria.

5. Evaluations should be done by reviewers with first-hand knowledge. If you are evaluating an employee, you should have first-hand knowledge of that employee's performance. If a supervisor changes just prior to evaluations, the new supervisor should note on the evaluation that it is being done based on limited knowledge and information (if the former supervisor is unavailable to complete the appraisals).

6. Make sure the evaluation covers the entire evaluation period. Do not let your evaluation suffer from "primacy," the overstatement of a single failure or accomplishment; or "recency," focusing only on the most recent

conduct during the appraisal period. You must make notes regarding the good and the bad throughout the appraisal period to ensure that your evaluation reflects the totality of the employee's performance.

7. Avoid the tendency to occupy the middle. To avoid confrontation or controversy, supervisors tend to lump employees toward the middle. Juries take "satisfactory" or "average" ratings seriously. Such ratings make it difficult to prove that an employee subsequently terminated or denied promotion for "poor performance" was really a poor performer.

8. Involve Human Resources or higher management in the process. Appraisals should be reviewed by someone other than the immediate supervisor before it is shared with the employee. This will guard against supervisory comments that might be improper or misconstrued as biased or unfair. Doing this allows any differences of opinion between managers regarding the employee's performance to be resolved before it is shared with the employee. It also ensures that supervisors are not making up their own rules for completing performance appraisals.

9. Allow the employee to appeal. The opportunity to appeal gives an objective, balanced and fair-minded approach to performance appraisals. If an employee cannot appeal the performance appraisal internally, you are giving the employee no choice but to look externally for help, i.e., the EEOC, a union, etc.

10. Keep evaluations confidential. Because of the potential for defamation actions, the physical document as well as the information contained within should be confidential and shared only with managers who have a need to know.

Performance appraisals are a pain. There may be organizations that do them well, but I have not seen many. Management consultant W. Edwards Deming is quoted as calling performance appraisals one of the seven deadly diseases of management.[16] Mr. Deming is correct. Performance appraisals can cause conflict, anxiety, headaches, nausea, and can lead to hurt feelings, de-moralization and lawsuits. That sounds like a disease to me. Regardless, there are still going to be organizations that require them or want you to do them. The best you can do is to conduct accurate, job-related performance appraisals that are meaningful and constructive for your employees.

For your consideration:

a. What can you do to ensure your performance appraisals are accurate?
b. What is the value of a performance appraisal?

## Taking the Hesitation Out of Documentation

Your employee, Emma, has developed a habit of being 15 – 20 minutes late reporting to work. You have brought this to her attention twice over the last three weeks but the problem has persisted and perhaps gotten even worse. What do you do?

You take corrective action and when taking corrective action with employees, your job as a manager is:

1. To use the skill and expertise necessary to effectively change the employee's behavior/performance.
2. To make sure your actions are such that the risk of a lawsuit against your organization is minimized. This risk is minimized by documenting what you are doing so that later a more evil motive cannot be attributed to your action(s).

Here are some points to consider on documentation:

1. Do it. Many times when I have asked a manager if he/she has documented a situation, I am told that yes, there is a lot of documentation, only to find that the documentation consists of notes to a file and the employee has been given nothing in writing; this does nothing to help the situation. While most managers like to think of themselves as being positive and nurturing, there is a point at which a manager not confronting an employee's poor performance/behavior ceases being positive and nurturing, and becomes an enabler.
2. Do it in a timely manner. There are psychological and legal truths that must be considered here. If you are going to praise or reprimand, it must be done in close proximity to the event that precipitated the praise or reprimand or the effect is diminished significantly. This is from Psychology 101 – the reward or punishment must closely follow the precipitating event. From the legal perspective, taking action too far removed from the precipitating event will only give a plaintiff's attorney an opportunity to claim that the action taken was

pre-textual (not for the reason you stated). Acting in a timely manner is critical.
3. Do it to everyone who needs it. The mistake many executives make is to think that other high-level managers (read executives) are above getting warnings or memos about their performance. Not so. The higher the level of the person filing the lawsuit, the more the lawsuit will cost. Your organization is going to need the same ability to defend its employment decisions with executives as it does with any other employee. Documentation in the form of written warnings is always an asset.
4. The goal is to change behavior, and the documentation is a by-product of pursuing that goal. The documentation is essential from a legal perspective but, if you are successful in changing Emma's behavior and no further action is necessary, there will be no legal issue with which to deal. If you are going to have any potential for success in changing behavior, you must successfully communicate to Emma: a) what she is doing wrong, i.e., the difference between expectations and actual performance; b) what she needs to do to do it right; and c) what will happen if she does not make the necessary corrections (this could be either a statement of potential outcomes related to the performance/behavior, it could be sanctions that may be taken, or both). Thus a document that covers the above (a – c) will be a good source to illustrate that whatever employment action was taken was done for legitimate reasons.
5. Remember due process. While most people could not give you a concise dictionary definition of the term it is something that we all inherently understand. In this context, it is making sure that the employee's side has been heard. Employees have an unerring sense for knowing when this has been violated. The example of due process abuse that I usually cite is when the manager calls an employee into his/her office, asks the employee for his/her side of the story, and then, after hearing the employee's side (but at that same meeting), the manager pulls out of the desk drawer a written warning to give to the employee. The employee then realizes that telling his/her side of the story was a joke; the manager had already decided what to do. In Emma's case, if she has a disabled child that she has to get into school

every morning, you would definitely want to know that before you take any kind of punitive action.
6. Consider the tone. Whether it is a verbal counseling or a written warning, there is no need to get ugly. The tone with which the message is delivered (written or verbal) can cause the content of the message to go unheard, which undermines the ability to change behavior. Remember also that your memo may be read (or that your verbal counseling may be quoted) by people outside of your area, perhaps even outside of your organization.
7. Get signatures. I have been in several situations where a memo, which by all other standards is a well done written warning, is not signed by either party. In this light, the unsigned memo looks glaringly sterile—it looks as though it was never executed and that is what the plaintiff's attorney usually asserts. You must sign or initial a written warning memo and either obtain the employee's signature or write on the memo that the employee accepted the memo but refused to sign acknowledging receipt. After all, the point is to communicate to the employee and if need be, to be able to prove that you communicated to the employee.
8. Allow the employee to respond. It is not unusual for an employee to want to write a response to the written warning. This is good; let them write an epistle if they like—it is both an emotional release for the employee as well as an opportunity to get their side in writing which lessens the chance that the story will evolve. Hopefully, you have done your due diligence so that you learn no new factual information as a result of the employee's response. Include the employee's response with your memo when you send it to the employee's official file in HR.
9. Consider the employee's state of mind as he/she leaves your office. At the end of the counseling session you must express confidence in the employee's ability to do the job/change the behavior. Managers do no good if an employee is given a verbal bashing and then turned loose to go take care of customers/clients and interact with co-workers. Having said that, you do not want to go so far that you discount what you have previously said (employees hate mixed messages). Be fair, control your emotions, know your facts as well as possible be-

forehand, do not make personal attacks and then let the employee know that you value him/her and have confidence that you will see a positive change, i.e., "I regret that I have had to conduct a counseling session with you but I am confident that you can take the feedback that I have given you and make some positive changes. I will be here to support you in any way that I can."

Having to give a written or verbal warning to an employee is unpleasant. But, two final points: a) Managing Emma's punctuality (performance) is a critical part of your role as a manager; and, b) If it were not for Emma's behavior/performance, you would not be taking such an action. Following this chapter is an example of a written warning that might be given to Emma.

For your consideration:

a. Why does documentation need to be in the form of a memo to the employee?
b. What kind of evil motive could be attributed to your actions if you do not produce documentation?

## Written Warning Example

Date: 10/15/20XX
To: Emma Who
From: Sam Manager
Regarding: Punctuality

On September 12, I had a conversation with you regarding your punctuality. At that time, I pointed out that we open at 8:00am, and that you need to be here ready to start work at that time. Since that conversation, you have been 15 – 20 minutes late on Sept. 15 and 22 as well as on Oct. 5 and 14 [or you can list the actual times for each date].

This tardiness places a burden on your co-workers who have to cover for your absence and on our customers who are inconvenienced by our inability to provide full service. Your job is critical to customer service, and you must be punctual.

If there is any way that I can assist you, please let me know. It is my expectation that you will make whatever adjustments need to be made so that you can show an immediate and continued improvement in your punctuality. I must inform you that should there be additional tardiness you may be jeopardizing your continued employment. I believe that you are capable of making whatever adjustments are necessary and I look forward to working with you.

Employee Comments:
Employee Signature:
Manager Signature:

## Verbal versus Written Warnings

To get even more specific about documentation, let's look at the two primary types:

Verbal Warnings

1. These should be used when an employee initially fails to meet behavioral and/or performance standards.
2. Do your fact finding first. This includes talking to the employee to get his/her side of the story before you give any kind of warning.
3. The verbal warning should include:
   a. A description of the behavior/performance that is unacceptable
   b. Positive suggestions for improvement
   c. Consequences of failure to correct problem
4. Stay in the coaching and counseling mode. Try to find out why the employee's performance or behavior is unacceptable and help the employee plan for a change.
5. Do not give the employee a written document for a verbal warning. You may document that you gave the warning in your notes (see Make a Note of It). You should have talking points that you use to speak to the employee to ensure that you stay on point, and these talking points will serve as your documentation that the warning occurred.
6. The verbal warning may be of limited value as documentation; however, if it changes behavior or improves the performance, then you have accomplished your goal.

Written Warnings

1. These should be used for a more serious offense, or when the employee's response to a verbal warning is not sufficient. You do not necessarily have to give a verbal warning before you can give a written warning.
2. Do your fact finding first. This includes talking to the employee to get his/her side of the story before you give any kind of warning. Do

not give an employee the written warning at the same meeting in which you do fact finding.
3. Message – Use the "What if I got it" test. Does it make sense? Is it appropriate?
4. Review the warning for:
   a. Tone – do not get personal, insulting, or nasty
   b. Content – do not bring up a laundry list of the employee's sins
   c. Clarity – will it make sense if read by an outsider?
5. Have the written warning reviewed by HR or your manager
6. The written warning must be signed by all parties; then it has great value both as a behavior modifier as well as documentation.
7. You can be sure that a jury will believe that if it isn't written down, it didn't happen!
8. What about documentation by e-mail? Performance management by e-mail is not generally accepted as a best practice in the management of people. It can be done as a follow-up to a meeting but, as a sole means of communication to an employee, it is viewed by the employee as what it is – a cop-out.

For your consideration:

a. Why shouldn't you give an employee a written document for a verbal warning?
b. Which is more effective, a verbal or written warning?

## Make a Note of It

A manager comes to see me about an employee who has, according to the manager, had a performance problem for some time. The manager explains to me what the employee has done or not done for the past several years that forms the basis for the manager's conclusion that the employee must be given the opportunity to work elsewhere. Given that the employee is in at least one protected class, I ask the manager what documentation she has that would demonstrate that she has communicated to the employee that his performance is deficient. (Even if the employee were not in a protected class, I would ask that question because that communication to the employee would be the right thing to do.) The manager sheepishly admits that she has no proof that she has communicated anything to the employee about his performance.

How do you write something down, and when do you do it?

Anytime you have to say anything of significance to an employee about his/her performance (or behavior) you need to make a note of it. If the incident does not rise to the level of requiring a written warning, there should be a notation made in your day planner, journal, etc., that you spoke to the employee and what was said.

Example of such a note:

*"Julie was late in setting up the spreadsheet I had asked her to do. I reminded her, and she had it to me this afternoon."*

Now, if there are no further problems, the note becomes an artifact. However, if Julie continues to have performance problems, you can then reference in the subsequent written warning that you have made previous coaching efforts (citing date and incident) regarding her being late with work.

Documentation by writing a note to the employee's file does not have the same value of a written warning to the employee, and it cannot be done in lieu of a written warning when the time comes to give the employee a written warning. The two means of documentation serve different purposes. Documentation by making a note of it is by far the easiest means of documentation for the manager; there is no confrontation with the employee, which a written warning sometimes causes, and, even with its limited value, it is better than no documentation at all. It is documentation that there was an issue, and you did some coaching.

So when do you go all the way and issue the employee a written warning? When there is a significant critical incident or when repeated verbal counseling with the employee is not effective. Making a note of an incident is a first step; but it is a first step that may help an employee get back on track.

For your consideration:

a. Which is the more difficult for you to do: coaching the employee or making a note that you did? Why?
b. What does making a note of it really accomplish?

# Termination of Employment – It Happens

When someone comes to me with the idea of terminating someone, it is usually based on one of the following:

A reduction in force (RIF) – the person(s) is being terminated because of a downturn in business or a function that is being outsourced or is no longer needed. It is no fault of the person involved.

A critical incident termination – this is a termination because the employee engaged in stealing, cheating, fighting, etc. – some act that is grounds for immediate termination.

A chronic situation termination – this is a termination where the employee has had prior warnings regarding performance or behavior, has not improved and now warrants termination.

Terminating the employment relationship with an employee is never easy but is the responsibility of management. But for the performance/behavior of the employee, you would not have to take such action; therefore, termination is not normally an action that should heap guilt on the manager. Here are some very important points to consider when faced with the reality that an employee may be facing termination of employment:

1. If you have an HR person, always consult with him/her before any termination. HR is not necessarily the final authority, but HR's role is to act as consultant and clearinghouse.
2. Thoroughly investigate the events leading to the termination. You must know all of the facts before the termination meeting is held.
3. Evaluate with HR the risk of litigation. Is the employee:
    a. Older than 40 years of age?
    b. Pregnant?
    c. Disabled?
    d. A minority or different race or gender than you or the other decision makers?

4. Is this a long-term employee? This means the employee may receive additional consideration.
5. Review the employee's file. If this is a chronic situation, is there documentation in the file?
6. Does documentation or evidence support termination? The word "documentation" means memos (written warnings) from you to the employee telling the employee what he/she is doing wrong, what he/she needs to do to improve, and what will happen if he/she does not. Evidence may be circumstantial or physical such as work-products, e-mails, etc. Evidence is good but, if I had to choose, I would prefer to have the good documentation. Having both is even better.
7. Has the employee recently filed a worker's compensation claim, harassment or discrimination claim? This could give rise to claims of retaliation. It doesn't mean you cannot terminate his/her employment if such a claim has been filed but you want to know and make sure everyone with a need to know is aware and has considered this fact.
8. Has the employee recently complained about improper activity within the organization, or raised a safety or pay issue? (again, termination could be viewed as retaliation)
9. Has the employee recently taken FMLA or military duty leave? (also possible retaliation)
10. Have other employees committed the same offense and not been fired? The key is to be able to explain why there has been a difference in treatment (if there has been) and how that has been handled; hence, the need for using HR as a clearinghouse.

You will want to be able to show that the decision to terminate a person's employment was made as a result of rational, deliberative thought between 2 or more members of management. It is never easy, and it is not fun, but when it has to be done, be prepared and do it as well as it can be done.

For your consideration:

a. If an employee has to be terminated due to performance/behavior, is the termination more the fault of management or the employee?
b. Why is it so important to have the documentation?

## The Termination Meeting

The only meeting that managers dread more than the performance appraisal meeting is the termination meeting. Some points to consider about the termination meeting:

1. Have another manager or HR staff in the meeting with you.
2. Tell the employee why he/she is being fired. Be clear and concise. You do not have to put it in writing (although some states do require this).
3. If you are unsure about what you plan to say, or fear that you may encounter resistance, consider writing a script. Not something that you will read verbatim but bullet-points that will help you stay on track.
4. Do not argue or apologize. Now is not the time and due process must have occurred prior to this meeting.
5. Avoid getting into any prolonged conversations. The time for debate has passed.
6. Do not counsel the employee or give advice at this time; it is too late for that.
7. Do not make any mention of protected class such as race, color, religion, national origin, sex, pregnancy, age or disability.
8. Do not mention any legal rights the employee has exercised such as taking FMLA, filing a worker's comp claim, or complaining about harassment, discrimination or working conditions.
9. Explain benefits that the employee will receive or that will be withheld.
10. Explain when the employee will receive the final paycheck.

The employee is uncomfortable; you are uncomfortable; it is an uncomfortable situation. But do not make it any more personal than it has to be. In other words, refrain from any personal attacks or comments and treat the employee with respect. You might say something like:

"I regret that this meeting is necessary. I must inform you that, effective immediately, your employment with our organization is being terminated. This is as a result of your performance problems for which you have received coaching and written warnings. You will need to speak to Mr. Smith in Human Resources regarding the final disposition of your pay and benefits."

All of what you just said must be true in order for you to say it. That is, you did coach and give warnings to the employee.

I have often found that employees were mad after being terminated, not so much because of the termination, but because of the manner in which they were treated by their manager, who, mere days ago, may have still treated them like a human being. So, look the employee in the eye, treat him with respect, and consider how you would want to be treated if you were in the same situation.

For your consideration:

a. What do you think is important to do or say in a termination meeting to preserve the terminated employee's dignity?
b. Why would it be important to preserve the terminated employee's dignity?

# Section Three

# People Selection

## Management Sense and People Selection

Common sense does not work at all when it comes to people selection. Many people use what they call their intuition to make hiring decisions. If you have intuition that you are aware of, pay attention to it, but do not rely solely on it when making hiring decisions. It just might sound a little weird if you have to defend your hiring decision in court and your intuition is all you have as your defense. You might want to have your psychic there to help your lawyer!

There is nothing in our common sense that tells us how to write minimum qualifications, how to analyze a job in order to write behavioral interview questions, or how to make a non-sexist, non-racist selection. Yet, many managers rely only on their common sense to make hiring decisions.

Common sense is really no sense at all when it comes to making management decisions. It takes understanding and applying Management Sense to know what to do to hire the person who is the most qualified for the job and to be able to defend that decision if it is questioned by someone internally (your boss) or externally (the Equal Employment Opportunity Commission).

In this section we will look at topics intended to enhance your Management Sense of people selection.

## Why Making Good Hires is Critical

Hopefully, you hear all the time how important it is to hire the right person for the job. If not, let me tell you – it is critical.

1. One day you will be gone, and the people you hired will be one of the ways in which you are remembered. It may not be right, but you will be remembered more for your bad hires than your good hires.
2. Your day-to-day aggravation and frustration level as a manager will be determined to some degree by the people that you hire.
3. You are going to spend about as many hours in a week with the people that you hire as you do with your family. (This is not a good excuse for hiring your family.)
4. The people you hire are the people who will or will not get things done. The quality of the people that you hire has a significant impact on the success and future of your department and your organization.
5. Since hiring is a big part of a manager's job, your performance rating will be determined (or at least it should be) to some degree by the quality of work produced by the people that you hire.
6. Every hiring decision that you make is a decision that exposes your employer to the risk of potential litigation with significant potential monetary damages. And not just every hiring decision, but every applicant you consider is also a risk factor since any applicant who is not hired could file a complaint.

Making a hiring decision is not a decision that you should ever take lightly. It should be a decision based on:

1. Careful consideration of the attributes needed for the job
2. A carefully planned hiring process
3. Job-related reasons for the hire that you can justify
4. Management Sense

For your consideration:
a. What do you think is the most critical outcome of making the right hire?
b. Upon what information do you normally make hiring decisions?

## Hiring Procedures – Got Any?

Is your organization large enough to have hiring procedures such as job posting? If you do have them, are they ever ignored? I would be willing to bet that they sometimes are and that most of the violations can be characterized by just one example:

While the job opening is still a gleam in the manager's eye, the manager discusses it with the person he thinks would be a good fit in the job. Subsequently, that person is put in the job. As a result, other qualified internal or external applicants will not be given genuine consideration because the job was essentially filled from the get-go.

Following your hiring procedures in letter and in spirit can produce measurable benefits:

1. Hiring decisions that you can defend. Nobody wants to be in the situation of having to testify that normal employment procedures were not followed; it is an uphill struggle from there.
2. A more diverse workforce. Hiring those you know only perpetuates your current demographic profile, which does not create a diverse workforce (unless you are friends with a highly diverse group of people).
3. You hire the best, most qualified applicant. Hiring in too small a circle can cause your hiring to become provincial. You need to look at what the world outside has to offer and hire the best, most qualified people that are available.

Most people who do not follow hiring procedures make that decision because they know who they want to hire, and they do not want to, or see no need to, open up the process. That is exactly the problem. The process is most fair, most defensible and most beneficial when it is transparent. It may be that the pre-selected individual is the most qualified individual and is ultimately hired, but, in the interest of defensibility, diversity and best practices, you should still follow your own procedures in letter and in spirit.

If your organization does not have hiring procedures, hopefully this will help you to see the need to develop even basic procedures. It is better to have some kind of written procedures so that even, if you have just a handful of managers, they know what to do and have guidelines for acting in a consistent manner. Even organizations with as few as 15 employees can be subject to claims of discrimination through the EEOC.

For your consideration:

a.  In your opinion, which is better for your organization – having no written hiring procedures or having something in writing?
b.  Why do some managers prefer to ignore hiring procedures whether they are in writing or not?

## Hire the Best People You Can Find

Once I had some managers come to see me to ask for my help in dealing with an employee who was not performing. I asked my usual litany of questions, the first being how long had the employee been with them. I was told 15 years. I asked when had the employee's performance started to decline, and I was told that it had never been acceptable. In fact, the managers told me that they had received a bad reference on the employee before hiring, but had hired him anyway. At least they were honest.

Managers' mistakes in hiring new employees can come back to haunt them. Many managers think that they can judge a good employee just by chatting with someone—big mistake. Ideally, whom you hire should be based on one thing and one thing only—a person's ability to do the job.

How can you determine a person's ability to do the job? I will go into more details later, but for a big-picture perspective, here is an overview of the interviewing and selection process:

1. Know what the job requires – knowledge, skills and abilities. If you cannot see the target, you cannot hit it. Know what you are looking for and make sure the "what" is job related.
2. Come up with questions that will tell you whether the applicant has the mix of knowledge, skills and abilities that you are seeking, questions that will bring the target into focus.
3. Ask your question and then listen. The 80/20 rule applies here – you should listen 80% of the time in an interview. To learn about an applicant you must ask good questions and actively LISTEN.
4. Hire the person whose responses indicate that they have the best knowledge, skills and abilities.
5. Make your decision, analytically and without bias, based solely on the degree to which the applicant meets or exceeds the minimum qualifications for the job.
6. If a reference gives you anything but positive information, take a second, hard look.

All of the above is to direct you toward hiring the person best qualified for the position. And, you should always be prepared to defend your decision, whether you are defending it to an internal source (your boss) or an external source (the EEOC).

For your consideration:

    a. How frequently do you really make hiring decisions based only on a person's ability to do the job?
    b. What do you actually do to prepare for the interview and selection process?

## The Maximum on Minimum Qualifications

A city president of the bank I worked for told the regional HR person to hire his golfing buddy's daughter, Emily, as a teller. The HR person did as she was told. The minimum requirement for a teller was one year of experience in a job that required cash handling. Emily (a non-minority) did not meet the minimum qualification.

The bank (a federal contractor) was later audited by the OFCCP (Office of Federal Contract Compliance Programs) and this hire was discovered. (If your employer is not a Federal Contractor, the EEOC could conduct this same type of investigation based on a complaint of discrimination.) In the eyes of the OFCCP, hiring Emily meant all of the teller applicants the bank had rejected for not meeting the minimum requirement were now part of an affected class because the bank had violated its own hiring standards. This cost the bank almost $45,000 plus legal fees and some bad publicity as the OFCCP almost always issues a press release. (Again, a similar situation could occur between you and the EEOC if an applicant were to file a complaint alleging failure to hire based on a protected class.)

Minimum qualifications are among the most important words you may write that have to do with hiring. They may be known as minimum qualifications, job specifications or by some other term, but they describe the minimum knowledge, skills, education and experience a person must have to obtain a job.

We are not told by any government agency or any other outside entity what to write as minimum qualifications for our positions – we write them ourselves. Therefore, writing them well is an important way in which to manage the risks associated with hiring. Here are some important characteristics about minimum qualifications:

1. They must be the minimum of what you will hire, not ideal. You can always hire above the minimum qualifications; if you hire below

your own minimum qualifications, you have, in effect, voided them as the bank did in the example with Emily. At least that is most likely how an investigator from the EEOC or OFCCP will interpret that.

2. They must be bright-line, i.e., you can readily tell if a person meets this requirement. Another way of saying this is that they should be more objective than subjective. For example, requiring sales experience is not as bright-line as is requiring sales experience in the electronics industry.

3. They must be job related. One of the landmark cases in employment law (Griggs v. Duke Power Company) involved Duke Power Company requiring a high school diploma for a job where they eventually could not show a high school diploma was necessary. That requirement had an adverse impact on minorities and was deemed to be unlawful; minimum requirements must be job related. Rather than say a job requires a college degree (not even specifying what degree), say that the job requires specific skills and knowledge such as, for example, experience in cost accounting and ability to interpret financial statements.

4. They should be clear and precise. You will frequently see an ad requiring "3-5 years' experience." What if an applicant has six years? A range is not appropriate because it actually has limits on the front and back side. The statement should have read "A minimum of 3 years of experience is required…"

5. The minimum qualifications section of a job description is the section that employers most frequently have to defend. This is the section that determines whether a person does or does not get the job.

Anyone writing an employment ad usually takes the minimum qualifications directly from the job description or an employment requisition and places it in the job posting or advertisements. Here are some actual minimum qualifications and a suggested re-write:

1.a. Actual

"Computer literate. Accounts Payable work experience. Basic bookkeeping/accounting knowledge. Ability to work effectively with the general public. Good organizational, planning, communication and interpersonal skills. High School Graduate."

1.b. Re-written

"The applicant must be able to pass tests showing basic competence in MS Word and Excel. At least one year's experience working in Accounts Payable. Must be able to show evidence of basic bookkeeping/accounting knowledge."

1.c. Comments

When experience is called for, be specific about the type and the length—just remember you can always hire above the minimum qualifications but never below. Working with the public and organizational skills are good interviewing issues but vague criteria by which to screen. What is the value of a high school diploma if they meet the other criteria in the re-written qualifications? I am suggesting that it is best if you do not specify a general educational requirement (unless it is required for licensure, etc.), but instead, say what specific skills the applicant needs that may be obtained through a high school education.

2.a. Actual

"Bachelor's Degree preferred. Experience working with computers in a PC environment required. Experience with automated telemarketing systems is highly desirable as well as analytical skills for comparative data interpretation."

2.b. Re-written

"The applicant must have college-level course work in comparative analysis or at least one year of experience in a job requiring comparative data interpretation. Must be able to pass tests showing competence in MS Word and Excel. In addition, any experience with automated telemarketing systems is desired but not required."

## 2.c. Comments

Again, do not say you want a college degree unless you can back up that need with some specificity. "Working with computers" is very vague. What you want to know is whether they have done the same thing (or more) with computers that you will want them to do in this job. Are you really saying *any* "experience with automated telemarketing systems" or can you be more specific?

You must have something in the minimum qualifications against which you can compare the education and experience of the applicant and say, "Yes they have it" or "No, they do not," and at the same time not have any intentional or unintentional discriminatory impact on applicants. This means you must carefully and thoughtfully analyze the job and come up with the minimum knowledge, skills and abilities that are necessary to perform the job in a satisfactory manner, and then state those in a manner by which you can compare the knowledge, skills and abilities of applicants.

For your consideration:

a. How bright-line are the minimum qualifications for the jobs for which you hire?
b. What are the advantages of having well written, bright-line minimum qualifications for your jobs?

## The Benefits of Experience

When I review job descriptions for managers, I usually focus on the minimum qualifications and especially on the minimum requirement for work experience. The problem is not that managers want to require too much experience; generally it is that they do not require enough. They do not require enough experience quantitatively or qualitatively.

What I mean by quantitatively is the number of years of experience. This should be based on several factors. First, for the majority of work in the job, what are the time cycles involved? Does most of the work happen every day or at least within a month's time? If so, then a year's experience should be sufficient to know that someone has mastered the tasks associated with this job (remember, we are talking in terms of minimums here, you can and should always hire above your minimum). But, if the time cycle of tasks is longer and a majority of the tasks come up only annually, then you might want to require a minimum of three years.

Second, you need to also consider the complexity of the tasks. If it is a highly complex task, and is only done once per year, an employee with only three years' experience has only completed the task three times. Is that enough for you to be sure you have a truly competent person in the job? For this example, you might want to consider a minimum of five years' experience.

When I use the term qualitatively referring to experience, I mean a specific kind of experience. If you are going to hire a framing carpenter, you want to write in the minimum qualifications that the job requires experience not just in carpentry but in framing carpentry. Framing carpentry, like most jobs, has a set of knowledge, skills and abilities (KSAs) that are unique to that job. Specifying that you want a framing carpenter will not only help you to hire a person who can come in and immediately start framing, but it will also eliminate from your applicant pool all general carpenters. That is a good thing because it focuses your search on the best candidates, it eliminates the work of sorting through all of those applications and it reduces your potential exposure to liability by reducing the number of applicants.

Knowing what experience you need for a job to be performed and then finding the person with that experience is absolutely fundamental to the hiring process; doing so means you will get the most for your money in the shortest time frame after the person is hired. Most organizations have few, if any, jobs that are so unique that you cannot find applicants with the appropriate prior experience; therefore, you should not be so willing to take on a significant amount of on-the-job training by hiring a person without the necessary experience.

The benefits of experience are that if you can express the quantitative and qualitative levels of experience and then hire the person that meets those criteria, you are going to:

1. Have a more focused and productive applicant search.
2. Have a more competent, autonomous person in the job in the shortest time possible.
3. Look like you have good Management Sense.

For your consideration:

a. Upon what criteria do you currently base your quantitative experiential requirement?
b. What impact would hiring the person with the most relevant experience have on your hiring new employees?

## What Do I Ask During an Interview?

Notice I did not say, "What do I not ask during an interview?" I think most HR people are guilty of telling managers too much about what you cannot do and therefore leave you not knowing what you *can* do. I believe this section will give you some good direction on what you can do.

When I do training seminars on interviewing, I always ask people to tell me the most ridiculous interview question they have ever been asked. Here are some samples:

"If you took your eleven-year-old self to lunch, what would you talk about?"

"If you were a tree, what kind would you be?"

"Do you plan to have more children?"

"What method of birth control do you use?"

"What am I going to hate about you in six months?"

Some of these are not only ridiculous and contribute nothing to selecting the most qualified candidate; they could also be the basis of a complaint of discrimination. Men are rarely asked questions about children and birth control—if a female is asked those questions and for any reason does not get the job, she could legitimately assume the reason was her answer to the female-specific questions and file a discrimination complaint based on that.

The real purpose of an interview is to learn as much as possible about a person's past job performance and behavior on the job because this knowledge is the best indicator of what the person's future job performance and behavior will be. The way that you do that is by asking questions that will elicit information about the applicant's former job knowledge, job performance and on the job behavior.

Most people do not use questions that elicit usable information; they simply go over the application or resume with the applicant and verify that what the applicant put on that document is really there. This is a waste of everyone's time.

Now, before we get into what I believe to be the most productive kinds of questions, there are three types of questions that you should avoid, not because they are potentially discriminatory, but because the use of these questions is not a good employment practice. They do not give you the information you need to make an informed decision about whether a person can do the job and behave appropriately in the workplace.

They are:

1. Leading questions – questions that suggest an answer. Do you really want to be giving hints about what you want the applicant to say during the interview? A leading question would be, "You don't use illegal drugs do you?"
2. Hypothetical questions – questions that elicit a hypothetical answer. Unless you are trying to determine how creative an applicant is, these are a waste of time. An example of a hypothetical question would be, "You see a co-worker stealing something from the company. What do you do?" You are going to get a made-up answer.
3. Yes or no questions – questions that elicit a one-word answer. Granted, you will have to ask a few of these, but limit it to as few as possible. An example of a yes/no question you might have to ask would be, "Do you have the necessary licensure to perform this job?" An example of a yes/no question to avoid would be, "Have you ever done shift work?"

I know that suggesting you not use the three types of questions mentioned above may leave you with no questions to ask at all, and I do not want to do that. In my opinion, the best way to approach the interview is to use what is known as behavioral interview questions.

Behavioral interview questions are questions that compare actual work-related experiences of the applicant to the job for which the applicant is applying. Now, there is something powerful implied in that statement — you must know what is required to perform the job.

You must know the knowledge, skills and abilities needed by the applicant in order for him/her to perform the job in question. You must know these things or how else would you determine whether a person is qualified for the job? This information is normally found in the job description (see the section "The Maximum on Minimum Requirements").

To create your behavioral interview questions, you must first perform some simple job analysis. Stay with me — this is not scary. Let's take an Administrative Assistant position. Let's say the minimum requirements are:

- A minimum of three years of administrative assistant experience.
- Experience with and knowledge of spreadsheet and word processing software.

But also, in analyzing the job, you know that this person will be required to provide administrative support to three managers, will be required to work a great deal of overtime and must compose letters based on only general guidelines.

Therefore, you might come up with questions such as:

Tell me about the experience you have as an administrative assistant. *This may be on the resume but having someone describe this may lead to more accuracy in terms of what was actually done.*

Describe to me the duties that you performed in that role. *This question will give you insight into what the person has actually done and how it compares to what he/she would do for you.*

Tell me how you have used spreadsheet software in your previous jobs. *Ask for several examples. Without tipping your hand you can find out the extent to which the applicant has used this software.*

Tell me how you learned to use the spreadsheet (or word processing) software. *You are looking for either on-the-job learning or a more formal classroom learning experience.*

Describe a situation in which you have provided administrative support to more than one person. *That is what the prospective job calls for; if the applicant has never done it, or has a bad experience with it, that will be important.*

Tell me about a time where you have had to work significant overtime. *If he/she has done it in the past, there is a high probability that he/she can and will be able to do it in the future.*

Tell me about any experience you have had composing letters. *Again, the past is a strong predictor of the future. Better yet, have some written general guidelines that might actually be used on the job and have the applicant actually compose and type a letter within a given time limit.*

What does all of this yield?

1. An interview process that is highly valid.
2. An interview that is analytical and job related.
3. An interview that is non-racist, non-sexist in nature.
4. An interview that appears professional and impressive.
5. An interview that actually gives you information with which you can make a defensible decision.

After you write the questions for one job, you do not have to go through that process again unless there are significant changes in the job.

However, with each applicant, you need to write down significant, verbatim phrases that the applicant uses to answer the questions. Then you will have the questions that you asked and significant verbatim phrases that the applicant used to respond to your questions. This will provide you with very good documentation that can assist you in your decision-making process as well as provide a defense for your hiring decision, should you ever need it.

Behavioral interview questions require a little extra preparation on the front end, but it is well worth the effort in order to hire the most qualified person for the job. Asking interview questions based on job analysis helps to ensure you screen out those who should be and to screen in the one that should be hired.

For your consideration:

a. What is the worst interview question you have ever heard asked?
b. How are behavioral interview questions different from what you currently use?

## Hiring a Manager Is Not Like Hiring Anyone Else

I was working at the bank just before Y2K (remember that crisis?) when we realized that we were losing programmers at an alarming rate. We desperately needed programmers to deal with the impending Y2K doomsday. I hurried over to the bank's operations center to conduct focus groups with the 70 or so programmers we still had in order to determine the reasons we were hemorrhaging programmers.

The bottom line that came out of the focus groups was that the programmers loved their environment, their benefits were excellent and their salaries were adequate. They were leaving because of their management and because they could – they were in demand. The problem was that the small group of senior managers for this group was described by the programmers as moody, unfriendly, unpredictable and unapproachable.

I was told during these focus groups that when programmers passed one of the senior managers in the hall and spoke, the manager gave no response. If programmers went to their manager's office, there was no predicting whether the manager would be in a bad mood or a good mood. These managers had no business managing people.

The managers were also accused of favoritism because they took smoke breaks and ate lunch only with certain employees on a regular basis. Favoritism can easily become a charge of discrimination, i.e., the person you go on smoke breaks with gets the promotion, the best raise, etc. Even if the raise or promotion to your smoke buddy is deserved, you will have a greater burden to defend your decision.

To remedy the situation, the bank made immediate plans to conduct one-on-one management assessment and training. Some of the managers were able to change their behaviors; some did not and were transferred to non-management jobs.

While every hire is important, the hiring of a person to fill a management role is especially critical. Since it appears that the courts have placed an increasing amount of emphasis on the authority vested in a manager by the employer, it is incumbent upon the employer to see that the person hired as a manager knows how to properly use that authority and will not abuse or misuse it.

In addition to the normal good interviewing practices previously discussed, here are some things that must be determined in utilizing Management Sense to hire a manager:

1. Has he actually had experience supervising the work of others? How much, how long and at what level? Managing the work of others is really not something to learn on the job except in lower-level positions. (Management trainees should be started as lead workers or by supervising one or two employees.) Interview questions: "Tell me about your experience managing employees." "Give me an example of how you used positive reinforcement to motivate employees."

2. Has she had some formal training in supervision? Great managers are not born; they are developed through education and experience (by developing Management Sense). Experience is necessary but there are some things that must be covered in the classroom. Interview questions: "Tell me about the classroom training in supervision that you have had." "Tell me about the management skills that you may have learned from a mentor or previous manager and how you have applied those skills."

3. Does he have good people skills? This may be the most important attribute. Good people skills means being outgoing, being articulate while saying what needs to be said, sensing the needs of others and adjusting your behavior accordingly, being courteous and respectful of others and being a good listener. Interview question: "Give an example of a situation in which your people skills helped to resolve a conflict at work."

4. Is she technically competent in the field in which she will be supervising? Employees will be coming to her asking technical questions. Nothing causes a manager to lose credibility faster than not being able to answer these questions or giving wrong answers. Interview question: "Give an example of how your technical knowledge of the area for which you are interviewing has supported employees' efforts in your current job."

5. Does he have good judgment? Whether a person has good judgment is very difficult to ascertain but you can get insight into judgment by asking him why he did some of the things he may mention in the interview process. Again, it is better to ask about real experiences than hypothetical situations. Interview questions: "Tell me about a time when you had to take a disciplinary action with one of your employees." After the applicant responds, make sure you find out why was that action taken and what was the outcome.

6. Is she selfless and confident enough to develop her staff? Sometimes people in supervision are so selfish and insecure that they are reluctant to develop the employees that work for them because they think the employees would then be a threat to their job security. A confident manager does not have that worry, and she understands that the best manager is one who develops her people by sharing expertise, information and power. Interview questions: "Tell me about how you may have trained your employees to perform components of your own job." Or, "give me some examples of how you have helped to develop those who have reported to you."

7. Has he had experience in hiring? Ask about the experience, how many employees he hired and whether he had any prior training in interviewing and selection. One of the most important decisions any manager will make is that of whom to hire. More interview questions: "Describe your philosophy and approach to interviewing. If you have ever made a bad hire, how did it happen?"

8. Does she have an idea of what her area of supervision should look like? Ask this question on a micro and a macro level. The best management candidate will be able to articulate a vision regarding the details of processes as well as how her area should fit into the big picture. Interview question: "Describe a time when you were able to fulfill your vision for your area of responsibility."

9. Has he been in a situation where he had to manage multiple priorities? Most, if not all, management positions require managers who, like jugglers, can keep many balls in the air at one time and all the while

know which ones are glass and which ones are rubber. Interview question: "Give an example of a work situation where you had to manage multiple priorities and deadlines."

10. Does she have integrity? Integrity (knowing right from wrong and doing right) is a critical trait for a manager but one of the most difficult to determine in an applicant. Interview question: "Describe a situation where you observed a manager doing something you thought was wrong/unethical. What was your reaction?"

The people who will be managed by the manager you hire will either thank you or curse you for hiring the manager. Following these Management Sense guidelines will increase the odds that you will be thanked.

For your consideration:

a. How is the hiring of a manager treated differently from the hiring of a non-manager in your organization?
b. What do you think managers should be screened for in the hiring process?

## The Advantages of Job Posting

Charles is manager of his department. A key assistant, Beth, has resigned. Charles tells Stan, one of his up-and-coming employees, that he is going to be promoted to Beth's job. Wanda, the department's only minority employee, overhears this conversation. Wanda is qualified for the job Stan has just been given, but Charles did not consider Wanda, inquire about her interest in the job, or realize that she is qualified.

Charles tells HR that the job is filled by Stan and that it does not need to be posted—there is little that HR can do at this point since there is no desire for the organization's job-posting policy to be a sham. After Stan's promotion is announced, Wanda files an EEOC discrimination complaint based on race with the intention of going to federal court. Charles' organization may have real trouble on their hands. Why?

1. The organization's policy was to post jobs, and HR did not post the job (because the job was filled). The organization violated its own policy and, unless there is a bona fide business necessity, such a violation is always viewed negatively by outside investigators/auditors. The heart of the matter is not that HR did not post the job; it is that Charles offered the job to Stan without the job being posted. Is it OK to have someone in mind for a job before it is posted? Absolutely: just don't go too far in communicating to that person beforehand and keep an open mind. The fact is you might actually find a better candidate after the job is posted. Remember that any and all communications you have with an employee about a job offer may later have to be recounted, under oath, during a deposition or on a witness stand.
2. Because the job was not posted, the applicant pool included Wanda and every other employee in the company. Had it been posted, the applicant pool would have included only those who applied. The applicant pool would have included Wanda and every other employee in the company even in organizations where job posting is not a policy or practice.

3. The claim of discrimination will be difficult to rebut because Wanda's qualifications for the job were not even considered.

Lessons that can be drawn from this scenario:

1. If your organization has a job posting policy, do not make hiring decisions or job promises before a job is posted. Keep an open mind and post the job.
2. If you do post, post all open positions and do not make a sham of the job-posting process by posting jobs that are actually already filled.
3. Do not communicate hiring decisions (this includes making a job offer) before all qualified (internal) applicants are considered.

Why is job posting so important?

1. It provides opportunity to employees and, more importantly, the hope of opportunity.
2. It helps to develop people. When an employee posts for a job, you have an opportunity to see his/her interests and ambitions and then discuss what he/she needs to do to develop and fill in the educational or experiential gaps.
3. It can significantly reduce liability in promotion decisions.
4. It is an arrow that can be taken out of the quiver of organized labor because it is one of the first things they will promise to employees.

If it is the policy of your organization to post all jobs, could there ever be any legitimate exceptions to this policy? Yes, there can be, but the notion that your job opening is special is not one of them, nor is the fact that you are in a hurry to fill the job. Everyone feels that way, and therefore, those are not exceptions. A reasonable exception for not posting a job would be: a) to place an employee returning from an approved leave, or b) to place an employee who would otherwise be without a job through no fault of his/her own.

If your organization does not have a practice of posting or a policy for posting jobs, see if you can get permission to post any open jobs in your area. A good way to do this is to send an email or do a physical posting for everyone in your area and list at least a summary of the job and the minimum requirements. If you send an email, make sure all of your employees receive it and have access to email. Ask for a written response so you have a record of who applies and when. You should also put a closing date on the posting. Everyone has an equal opportunity to express their interest in the job this way.

For your consideration:

a. How well do you think the process works for considering internal applicants in your organization?
b. What do you think are the pros and cons of job posting?

## Internal Transfers – Don't Pass the Lemon

Hiring internally often results in better retention of employees. In addition, hiring internally means keeping people together, this often improves teamwork.

You have an opening for an assistant and an internal applicant named Julie applies. Julie meets the minimum qualifications, but you have heard through the grapevine that she has been a problem in her current department and is really trying to get out before she is fired. What can you do, and what are your responsibilities in an internal hire?

On an internal hire, like any hire that you make, you need to make sure that you:

1. Hire the right person for the right reasons. Have you looked at the internal applicant's employee file in HR or talked with his/her current manager? If you are a hiring manager, you can and should do both of these things. This is a part of the due diligence that is frequently overlooked. Hopefully you can obtain truthful information from your peer managers about internal employees. Talk to Julie's manager and also your HR manager to ensure that Julie is the real deal.
2. Make a decision based on job-related factors. We know internal applicants because we work with them, but you should not be hiring because he/she is a buddy, you think they need help, or you feel sorry for them. There are lots of things you can do for those people but promoting/transferring them for the wrong reason is not in your or your department's best interest.
3. Hire analytically and without bias. Complaints about internal hiring are among the hardest to defend unless the decision has been made analytically and without bias. That means analyzing whether the internal applicant is the most qualified based on a comparison of their knowledge, skills and abilities to the minimum qualifications for the job. "Without bias" means not letting any protected factor

(race, gender, age, etc.) influence your thinking of whether or not to promote or transfer the person.
4. Use your Management Sense to consider internal transfers. Internal hires can result in problems that are every bit as serious as external hires.
5. Do not become a victim of "Pass the Lemon". If it is an internal hire, look at internal files, talk to people that have experience with the internal candidate, talk to her supervisor. Make sure that you are not giving a new home to someone else's problem.

Employees who are a problem in one area should not be rewarded with a promotion or transfer. Also, keep in mind that if you transfer one employee with performance problems, how can you justify terminating the employment of the next employee with performance problems rather than allowing a transfer? The right reasons to promote or transfer would be that the person meets or exceeds the minimum qualifications for the open position and has a good record in their current job.

For your consideration:

a. What are your thoughts on allowing problem employees to transfer?
b. What do you think is the moral obligation of the lemon-passer to the hiring department?

## How to Avoid Hiring the Wrong Person

It sometimes happens that we hire the wrong person for the job, i.e., the person is not successful in the performance of that job. Lack of success can certainly be a function of the right person being mis-managed, but for purposes of this discussion I want to focus on the possibility the wrong person was hired.

In one of my hospital HR departments, I had an opening for a benefits analyst. This person paid benefit vendors, worked with employee benefit questions, etc., so I concluded the job needed someone with some accounts/payable experience.

I received a resume that appeared to have the skills and experience I was seeking and called the person in for an interview. Rhonda was a very attractive young lady, divorced with two young children. Bright, articulate and ready to go to work, I hired Rhonda after checking one of her job references, which said she was a good employee. Shortly after Rhonda was trained and up to speed, I started noticing things were not getting done correctly or on time.

After I caught her in a lie about whether she had done part of her job, I had to review some of her work and found that she had not completed important elements of her job for a significant period of time. I decided that was the end for Rhonda.

It can happen to the best of us. I asked myself, "Did I hire her because she was attractive?" "Did I hire her because she was divorced with two small children and I was being paternalistic?" "Did I hire her because she met the minimum qualifications and received a good reference?" "Did I hire her because of all of the above?"

Even when you do everything right it can turn out wrong. But, you significantly reduce the chances of it turning out wrong when you do everything right. Got that?

So, how is the wrong person sometimes hired?

1. Sometimes we are fooled. Even the best interviewers can be fooled, and it will happen eventually in your lifetime. "Happen eventually" assumes you are an effective interviewer; it will happen a lot if you are not. Hopefully, this is not a frequent occurrence.
2. We hire for the wrong reasons. We hire a person because we go to church with her; we know his parents; she is attractive; he attended the same school that we did; we were in the same fraternity/sorority; she presents well, etc. Or, we hire because we are desperate and just need somebody or have some other ulterior, non-job-related, motive. All of these are bad reasons (and ultimately indefensible reasons) upon which to base a decision to hire. Hiring for one of these wrong reasons frequently makes it that much harder to deal with the person after problems arise.
3. We do not know what we are looking for. If you have not done an adequate job of writing minimum qualifications, knowing the knowledge, skills and abilities to do the job well, you are shooting at a target that is completely out of focus.
4. We do not follow the simple formula: Know the job-related minimum requirements for the job, and then find the best person for the job that meets or exceeds the minimum requirements.

Your job is to hire the right person for the right reasons. It takes planning, preparation and careful execution of the plan. Hopefully, you will use Management Sense to improve your odds of making the right hire.

For your consideration:

a. Would you take a different approach to dealing with being fooled by an applicant versus having made a hiring error?
b. Which of the above situations is the more difficult?

# Section Four

# Application

## Employment Laws

OK, you might think employment law is awfully boring. But, employment law is really one of the most important foundations of Management Sense. You really have to have a basic knowledge of the laws that govern the workplace.

As much as we sometimes complain about the effects of various state and federal laws, imagine the chaos that would result if we were not a nation of laws. This thought certainly applies to the workplace. There are three things that really have an impact on how the workplace is governed: your organization's policies, your state laws and our federal laws. These things form a very critical part of the foundation of Management Sense.

Organizational Policies

You need to know your organization's written policies as well as its unwritten practices. Every organization is different and has different policies and practices for handling people situations. As a manager, you need to familiarize yourself with your organization's policies and practices and abide by them.

As a manager you are given a degree of power to enforce these policies. What you say and do to employees can create a commitment that your employer has to honor. Therefore, knowing your employer's policies will enable you to use your management power and discretion as your employer would have you to do. Doing this is usually very good for your career.

Your organization may not be large enough to have formal policies and procedures as I have pointed out before. However, that does not exempt you from compliance with applicable state and federal laws.

State Laws

Some states have few if any employment laws. Other states have a multitude of state laws regarding the workplace. There are even some cities that have employment laws. It is important, however, that you know what these laws are that affect your workplace and abide by them.

Federal Laws

There are many sources for information on the federal laws that govern the workplace. The important thing is that you must have some idea of what these laws are and how they affect the way you manage people in the workplace.

Some of the sources you might use to find out more about the federal employment laws are training from your employer, the Internet, books or videos.

## Putting All of This to Work

The thing about management training or management books is that they do absolutely no good unless the information imparted is actually instrumental in changing someone's behavior. In this case, it is you, the supervisor, manager, director, vice president, president, etc., that needs to accept that perhaps some of your management behaviors need to change. We all need to manage people more effectively. Not one of us is a perfect manager or ever will be. Hopefully, something(s) in this book made a connection with you, and you will improve in some way the way you manage and treat people.

In *Good to Great,* author Jim Collins points out that every company that transitions from good to great has as a leader during this period of transition, someone who has what Collins calls "Level 5" leadership traits.[17] Surprisingly, foremost among these traits is humility, the ability to be self-effacing and understated, but also with a strong desire to produce results.[18] As Collins makes the point, "more plow horse than show horse".[19] In other words a "Level 5" leader is a person who is able to effectively sublimate his/her ego to get the job done by working effectively through other people.

You must also be able to sublimate your ego in order to critically look at how you manage people (or to be able to really listen to others who provide you that valuable feedback) and then actually make changes in your behavior. It is very hard for most managers to accept that the way in which they presently manage people might not be the best way, and therefore, that they need to change. To change behavior like that is hard for managers because their ego tells them that the way they are treating people is the best way to do it. Or, it may be that their ego is so powerful the manager has not even considered what effect his/her management style is having on employees (the epitome of the management jerk).

For every action that you take, there is going to be a reaction from your employees. If you are going to be effective as a manager, you need to understand how that works and care about how that works. And, you must be willing to change your behavior if you expect the people that you manage to change theirs. Having and using Management Sense will show your employees that you respect them and that you are serious about being a good manager. Go put it to work.

## Endnotes

1. Daniels, Aubrey C. *Bringing Out the Best in People: How to Apply the Astonishing Power of Positive Reinforcement*. New York: McGraw-Hill Education, 2000, p. 10.

2. *Ibid*, p. 11

3. Brown, W. Steven. *13 Fatal Errors Managers Make: And How You Can Avoid Them*. New York: Berkley, 1987, p.52.

4. Peters, Thomas J. 1988. *Thriving on Chaos: Handbook for a Management Revolution*. New York: Knopf, 1988. 423-40. Print. As referenced in Leonard, Edwin C., and Raymond L. Hilgert. "Chapter 3." *Supervision: Concepts and Practices of Management*. Mason, OH: Thomson/South-Western, 2004. 79. Print.

5. D. Michael Abrashoff, Commander of the USS *Benfold* sits down with his new crew members and tries to learn something from them. As reported in Polly LaBarre, "The Agenda – Grassroots Leadership." *Fast Company* (April 1999), pp. 114+. As referenced in Leonard, Edwin C., and Raymond L. Hilgert. "Chapter 3." *Supervision: Concepts and Practices of Management*. Mason, OH: Thomson/South-Western, 2004. 79. Print.

6. Bohlander, George, and Scott Snell. *Managing Human Resources*. Mason: Cengage South-Western, 2006, p. 14.

7. Bazerman, Max H. *Negotiating Rationally*. New York: Free P, 1993. p. 10.

8. *Ibid*, p.13.

9. *Ibid*, p.15

10. Edward L. Harrison, "Why Managers Fail to Discipline". *Supervisory Management*. no. 4. April 1985

11. *Ibid*, p.153.

12. Buckingham, Marcus, and Curt Coffman. "Chapter 1." *First, Break All the Rules: What the World's Greatest Managers Do Differently*. New York, NY.: Simon & Schuster, 1999. 33. Print.

13. Goleman, Daniel, and Richard Boyatzis. "Social Intelligence and the Biology of Leadership." *Harvard Business Review* 9th ser. 86 (2008), pp.74-81.

14 Leonard, Edwin C., and Raymond L. Hilgert. "Chapter 4." *Supervision: Concepts and Practices of Management*. Mason, OH: Thomson/South-Western, 2004. 118. Print.

15 Charles T. Speth, II and Pavneet S. Uppal,"Evaluating Employee Performance without Creating Legal Liability". 2006 Workplace Strategies Seminar, Ogletree, Deakins, Nash, Smoak & Stewart, P.C., pp. 6-9

16 Deming, W. Edwards. *Out of the Crisis*. Cambridge, MA: Massachusetts Institute of Technology, Center for Advanced Engineering Study, 1986. Print, p. 98.

17 Collins, James C. "Chapter 2." *Good to Great: Why Some Companies Make the Leap--and Others Don't*. New York, NY: Harper Business, 2001. Print, p. 22.

18 *Ibid*, p. 22.

19 *Ibid*, p. 33.

# About the Author

Fred has an undergraduate degree from Auburn University and a graduate degree from the University of Alabama at Birmingham. He has been a professional in Human Resources for almost 35 years and has been a careful observer of management for all of that time noting the good and the bad. His human resources career path has included healthcare, banking and higher education.

Fred has also been an instructor in higher education for over a decade. He has taught courses in Human Resources Management, Supervision and also in Conflict Resolution/Negotiation. He has worked as a mediator for the EEOC and has been a speaker at a number of local, state and national conferences.

He is married to Janis, an advertising executive, and they have three children and two dogs. His hobby is playing guitar and pedal steel guitar.

CPSIA information can be obtained
at www.ICGtesting.com
Printed in the USA
LVHW092300310320
651840LV00003B/809

*présentées par*

Robert Winston Kretsch

*Polytechnic Institute of Brooklyn*

McGRAW-HILL BOOK COMPANY
New York St. Louis San Francisco Dallas Toronto London Sydney

# ACKNOWLEDGMENTS

The author wishes to thank the publishers, authors, and holders of copyright for their permission to reproduce the following literary works:
*Acte sans paroles I* by Samuel Beckett, Editions de Minuit.
"Scene I" from *La Cantatrice Chauve* by Eugène Ionesco, © Editions Gallimard.
"Parez, Dégagez" from *Gens Qui Passent* by Paul Margueritte, Librairie Ernest Flammarion.

IMAGES ET REFLETS LITTERAIRES

Copyright © 1967 by McGraw-Hill, Inc. All Rights Reserved. Printed in the United States of America. This book, or parts thereof, may not be reproduced in any form without permission of the publishers.

35491

Library of Congress Catalog Card Number 67-11457

1 2 3 4 5 6 7 8 9 10   HD   76 75 74 73 72 71 70 69 68 67